Paolo Petr

Fresh Pasta
my love

The best recipes
for tagliatelle, lasagna, orecchiette
and other types of traditional pasta

Editor
Roberto De Meo

Editing
Alessandra Pelagotti

Art direction
Constanza Di Gregorio

Page layout and cover design
Leonardo Di Bugno

Translation
Cristabelle Tumola

Photographs
Giunti Archive: p. 19; © Lorenzo Borri, Giovanni Petronio pp. 26, 27, 65, 73, 93, 98, 117; © Fotocronache Germogli pp. 33, 41, 45, 55, 89, 107, 113, 119, 123; © Foto M. Favi pp. 3, 20, 21, 25, 125;
© Fotocronache Germogli, Firenze, Italy: pp. 37, 59, 75, 79, 126;
© Robert Harding/Cuboimages, p. 53.

www.giunti.it

Via Bolognese 165 - 50139 Firenze - Italy
Via Dante 4 - 20121 Milano - Italy
First edition: april 2011

Reprint	Year
5 4 3 2 1 0	2015 2014 2013 2012 2011

Printed by Giunti Industrie Grafiche S.p.A. – Prato (Italy)

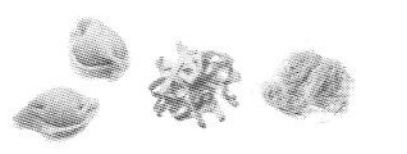

Contents

Introduction

We all have books that speak of famous homemade pasta dishes and probably every month read many recipes in cooking magazines and other sources. Now restaurants offer a wide variety of pasta flavored in the most imaginative ways and companies are meeting needs by rapidly delivering products that can be cooked in a few minutes. Dry pasta can be found ready-made, not just frozen, but also freeze-dried in packages—just toss it in the pan for a moment and you can have it in a snap.

Unfortunately, because of attempts at creativity and the desire to develop new recipes at all costs, the sense of proportion and taste has been lost, and there are no longer certain benchmarks.

Just try and search for recipes for Genovese pesto, pappardelle with rabbit, tonnarelli cacio e pepe, orecchiette with turnip greens, macaroni alla chitarra with lamb ragu or bolognese sauce.

I was only able to remember some of the most famous recipes, although I tried! These recipes always vary, so which are the right ones? Well, some are right, some are almost right, but unfortunately some are blatantly wrong.

It's for that reason that I wanted to gather in one volume the whole panorama of homemade pasta.

Paolo Petroni

The Origins

The term "pasta" (perhaps from the Greek *pastài*, meaning "flour mixed with a liquid") is so broad and vague that it is impossible to speak of its origins; if dough is any mixture of flour and water, boiled and flavored with various fat, cheese, meat or fish based sauces, we get lost in the maze of history of the cuisines from many countries.
Indeed, the first man-made pastas were, in all likelihood, "gnocchi" (or dumplings), large or small balls originally made of water and millet, sorghum and farro flours.
There is no doubt, however, that dried pasta was preceded by many centuries by fresh, and was made to have a long shelf life and therefore was ideal for transport.
The oldest evidence of the manufacturing of pasta dates back to the 4th century B.C. In an Etruscan tomb called "reliefs," near Cerveteri, frescoes have been found that clearly show all the ingredients and the tools to make dough: flour, a water jug, pastry board, rolling pin and even a cutting wheel to cut pappardelle or tagliatelle, or to make ravioli.
For the Etruscans, dough was considered noble food and was of great value, enough to be depicted in their tombs.
Many centuries later we find in the *Satires* of Horace (35 B.C.) and in Apicius's *De re coquinaria* (around 30 A.D.) numerous references to the terms *làganon* (in Greek) or *làganum* (in Latin), but it doesn't seem that they were referring only to delicious lasagna or tagliatelle, but also to a kind of broiled focaccia—a sort of current day "testaroli" from Pontremoli, perhaps the world's oldest pasta.

Fresh "Homemade" Pasta

Homemade pasta is unsurpassed; it is the most delicious of all, and is not remotely comparable to fresh industrial or artisanal pasta, but nowadays the quality has improved considerably.

Fresh pasta can be divided into:
- Egg pasta
- Eggless pasta
- Stuffed pasta
- Gnocchi

This book only deals with egg and eggless pasta.

EGGS

Grades and Standards. Today in the U.S., in stores you can find different types of eggs classified according to their size and quality. On each carton of eggs there is an official USDA Grade Shield, guaranteeing the processing and packaging of the eggs and that they meet the USDA's Standards, Grades and Weight Classes for Shell Eggs. Size indicates the minimum required net weight per dozen eggs, not the dimensions or how big the egg looks. Although some eggs may be a little smaller or bigger than other eggs in the same carton, it's the total weight of the dozen eggs that determines its weight class.

Minimum Net Weight Per Dozen
- Jumbo, 30 ounces
- Extra Large, 27 ounces
- Large, 24 ounces
- Medium, 21 ounces
- Small, 18 ounces
- Peewee, 15 ounces

Grade quality and size are not connected. Before eggs can be sorted by size they need to be examined for their quality, both inside and out (the appearance and condition of the egg shell) at the time the eggs are packed. There are three egg grade designations: AA, A and B. According to the USDA the egg grades are determined by the following:

- Grade AA eggs have whites that are thick and firm; yolks that are high, round, and practically free from defects; and clean, unbroken shells.
- Grade A eggs have characteristics of Grade AA eggs except that the whites are "reasonably" firm. This is the quality most often sold in stores.
- Grade B eggs have whites that may be thinner and yolks that may be wider and flatter than eggs of higher grades. The shells must be unbroken, but may show slight stains. This quality is seldom found in retail stores because they are usually used to make liquid, frozen, and dried egg products.

Fresh egg pasta purchased from supermarkets or gourmet stores contains about 1 1/2 pounds of eggs (interchangeable with "egg products" that are made from eggs in the form of liquid, concentrated, dried, crystallized, frozen, etc.), amounting to **about 4 eggs** per 2 1/4 pounds of flour, but to make real pasta dough it takes 10 eggs per 2 1/4 pounds of flour.
Speaking of eggs, it's necessary to mention that there are different traditions depending on the Italian region, with a precise pattern from north to south.
They range from Piedmont, where for taglierini, even as many as 30 egg yolks (egg whites are not used) are used per 2 1/4 pounds of flour. In Tuscany, certain traditions use only 2 or 3 eggs per 2 1/4 pounds of flour. Finally, in other regions, especially southern ones (but also in Liguria), where the pasta is usually short, the dough is even made without eggs.
The more eggs you put in the dough, the firmer it will be; if you put a small amount of eggs and a lot of water in it, the dough will be softer and less flavorful. Everything depends on local traditions, from the size of the pasta to the sauces used.

Flour

Flour is also important; usually soft wheat flour (*Triticum sativum*) is used, but not 00 (double zero) –which is suitable for desserts–it's best to use type 0 soft wheat flour. Today durum wheat flour (*Triticum durum*) can also be found in stores as "semolina"; it is not very suitable for pasta dough (even though industrial fresh tagliatelle often is made with durum wheat flour), if anything, a little of this flour (about one third) can be mixed with type 0.

Today, some local preparations also use special flours, such as farro or whole wheat.

Instead, for certain southern preparations (orecchiette, macaroni al ferretto and many others), it's necessary to use only whole wheat flour without eggs.

"Classic" Egg Pasta Dough

The classic egg pasta dough recipe, typical of Emilia Romagna (the undisputed motherland of homemade egg pasta), is a little complex to make, but the results are excellent.

I have seen this process done many times by expert hands, whose secrets I am revealing to all of you. Of course you can use a machine to make the dough, such as a food processor or mixer with a dough attachment (which would horrify housewives throughout Italy), but the dough will be a bit too smooth and will not hold its seasonings as well. In order to make tagliatelle and similar pasta, however, do not use electric pasta machines (they put too much pressure on the dough and are best suited to make bigoli or spaghetti). Instead, it's best to use traditional pasta machines in which the dough is first flattened and then cut with different width rollers.

Basic Egg Pasta Dough Recipe – *Serves 6*

- 3 1/4 cups type 0 flour plus extra for the working of the dough
- 4 medium eggs at room temperature

Work in a cool, draft-free room.
Mound the flour on a wooden pastry board. Add the eggs to the center (do not add any salt or oil).
Begin to knead with your fingertips, first breaking up the eggs and then bringing the flour from the edges to the center, a little at a time.
Continue to knead, first "wringing," then kneading the dough vigorously with the palms of your hands, using the weight of your body, starting first with the right wrist, then the left, continuing to alternate (it's a mistake to knead the dough using the strength of your arms, you need to use the whole weight of your body, using one hand at a time).
While kneading, add a little flour to the board from time to time. When you are halfway through kneading the dough, wash and thoroughly dry your hands (pieces of dry dough on your hands will ruin the rolling out of the dough).
Continue to knead for about 15 minutes, until the dough is smooth and elastic.
Let it rest on the counter, wrapped in plastic wrap, for about 20 to 30 minutes. Flatten out with a rolling pin (or machine).
Without too much force, roll the rolling pin back and forth with your hands outstretched and covered in flour and with the pastry board covered in a little flour also, so that the dough does not stick.
As soon as the dough starts to roll up onto the rolling pin, starting from the top, slide it down and in the opposite direction, flattening it out again, with the dough rolled up on the rolling pin, rotating it 90 degrees so that it is perpendicular to you and start over.
Continue flattening the dough until it becomes a very thin and perfect round (less than 1/8 inch thin).

Classic Sizes of Some Traditional Pasta Shapes

- Capellini or capelli d'angelo (angel hair): about 1/20 inch
- Taglierini, tagliolini or tajarin: about 1/10 inch
- Tagliatelline, tagliarelli: about 1/8 inch
- Roman fettucce, fettuccelle: about 1/4 inch

- Classic Emilian tagliatelle: about 1/4 inch (about 1/3 inch cooked)
- Classic Roman Fettuccine: about 1/3 inch
- Emilian maccheroni and pappardelle: about 1 inch
- Tuscan pappardelle: about 1-1½ inches
- Lasagna: about 4x6 inches
- Quadrucci: about 1/4 inch (cut again into small squares without rolling out the dough)
- Maltagliati: about 1/3 inch, with diagonal cuts (in order to form elongated triangles)
- Abruzzo sagne: diamond shapes with about 3/4 inch sides

Colored Pasta

Pasta often comes in different colors, such as red, green and black. To make these colors, a normal pasta dough with different ingredients added to it is used.

Red pasta is made by adding a heaping tablespoon (per 3 1/4 cups flour) of double concentrated tomato paste dissolved in a little warm water to the dough.

Green pasta is made by adding about 1/2 pound spinach – or Swiss chard or nettle (per 3 1/4 cups flour)–that has been boiled, drained and chopped, then passed through a food mill or put in a food processor, to the dough (you can also use a handful of basil, finely chopped in a food processor).

Black pasta is made by adding two black ink cuttlefish bladders to the dough.

Yellow pasta is made by adding about a pinch of saffron that has been dissolved in a little warm water to the dough.

Brown pasta is made by adding a heaping tablespoon of unsweetened cocoa powder to the dough.

You can also make other colored pasta using about 3/4 cup of pureed **porcini mushrooms** sautéed in olive oil, olives in brine, **artichokes** sautéed in olive oil, boiled **red beets** (or a glass of beet juice). For all of these preparations, use 2 **eggs** (instead of 4), per 3 1/4 cups flour.

Variations

The above procedure is perfect, but there are also some variations in regional specialties. In any case, I do not recommend adding oil to the dough (it would facilitate the process) and above all the salt would "cook" the fat of the eggs and flour.

• You can use 1 whole egg plus 1 yolk per 1 cup flour (such as in Piedmont).
• You can use only 2-3 eggs per 4 cups flour plus cold water (such as for pappardelle and some Tuscan tortelli).
• You can mix soft wheat flour and durum wheat flour.
• Southern pasta types, such as orecchiette, are made without eggs and only with durum wheat flour.
• If you use a **pasta maker**, it's not necessary to work the dough for a long time, just pass it through the machine, decreasing the setting from time to time.

Eggless Pasta Dough

Fresh pasta made only with flour and water is mostly typical of southern regions, but has spread to other ones. Usually it's made with durum wheat flour, known as semolina, but many recipes include, type 0 soft wheat flour.

BASIC EGGLESS PASTA DOUGH RECIPE – *Serves 6*

- 3 1/4 cups type 0 durum wheat flour (semolina), plus extra for the working of the dough
- Salt

Work in a cool, draft-free room.

Mound the flour on a wooden pastry board. Add a pinch of salt and 1 cup room temperature water.

Begin to knead with your fingertips and bring the flour from the edges to the center, a little at a time, making sure not to break the walls of the well.

Continue to knead, first "wringing," then kneading the dough vigorously with the palms of your hands, using the weight of your body, starting first with the right wrist, then the left, continuing to alternate (it's a mistake to knead the dough using the strength of your arms, you need to use the whole weight of your body, using one hand at a time).

When the dough is smooth and no longer sticks to the hands (about 10 minutes of kneading), flatten it out with a rolling pin, with the help of a little flour and immediately cut it into your desired pasta shape.

Principal Pasta Types Made Only with Water and Flour

NAME	REGION	FLOUR	SHAPE	TYPICAL SAUCE
Bigoli	**Veneto**	Soft wheat or whole wheat	Large spaghetti al torchio, about 1/8 inch in diameter	Duck or fresh water sardines
Filei, fusilli al ferro, ferretti, minnicchi	**Calabria, Basilicata**	Durum wheat	Cordoncini, about 2 1/3 inch long wrapped around a knitting needle	Meat sauce and breadcrumbs, tomato sauce
Lagane, laganelle	**Apulia**	Durum wheat	Pappardelle, about 3/4-1 inch wide	Vegetable sauce or sauce with chickpea or bean puree
Malloreddus or gnoccheddi sardi	**Sardinia**	Durum wheat, with a little saffron	Very small and ridged gnocchetti	Tomato and sausage sauce
Orecchiette, cicatelli, cavatelli, strascinati etc.	**Apulia**	Durum wheat	Round and concave	Broccoli rabe, braciole ragu
Pici	**Tuscany**	Soft wheat	Wide and quite short spaghetti	Aglione (garlic sauce), duck or sausage ragu
Pizzoccheri	**Lombardy, Valtellina**	Soft wheat and buckwheat	Short tagliatelle	Butter, cheese and vegetables
Trofie	**Liguria**	Soft wheat	Sticks rolled up around themselves	Basil pesto

How to Cook Pasta

Pot

Use a high-quality pot with a thick bottom to guarantee an even and consistent heat. A large pot is best–I suggest a 2 gallon pot, both 10 inches wide and high, for a 4 person portion of pasta. I do not recommend using special pots made for pasta, with a pasta strainer inside–they extend the cooking time, reduce space for the pasta, make unnecessary noise and don't drain easily.

Water and Salt

Boil 4 1/4 cups water per 1/4 pound pasta (for 4 people use 1 pound pasta and 1 gallon water). As soon as the water starts to boil, add 1 heaping teaspoon coarse salt per 4 1/4 cups water (for 4 people use about 1 1/2 tablespoons). I also recommend adding a tablespoon of olive oil to prevent the pasta from sticking.

Cooking

Cook for a couple of minutes and stir the pasta. Increase the heat in order to maintain the boil and stir with a wooden fork so that the pasta becomes fully immersed in the water as quickly as possible. Continue to stir as the pasta cooks. As soon as the pasta is almost cooked, soft and firm (it only takes a few minutes for egg pasta), drain it quickly in a large colander and transfer the **still very wet** pasta, surrounded by a thin layer of water, into a serving bowl that has been **warmed** with boiling water or into the skillet with the sauce. Never stop the cooking with cold water and never cook the pasta halfway and then cook it again when you are ready to serve it–those are two sure ways to ruin pasta.

Sauce

Immediately combine with the sauce in a serving bowl and toss well. If the pasta needs to be sautéed or "whisked" in the skillet, cook it for 1 minute less than needed; in other words, cook until it's very *al dente*.

Typical Regional Pasta

REGION	FRESH PASTA
Valle d'Aosta	Chestnut fettuccine, squash, buckwheat and potato gnocchi
Piedmont	Biavetta, taglierini or tajarin, corzetti, crosets, dunderet, rabaton
Liguria	Battolli, bricchetti, corzetti, fregamai, gasse, lasagne, mandilli de saea, piccagge, preagge, trofie
Lombardy	Bardele, pizzoccheri, bigoli
Trentino-Alto Adige	Canederli, knödel, fregoloti, talleri, spätzle
Veneto	Bigoli, lasagne, paparele, subioti, tirache, torchiatini
Friuli Venezia Giulia	Lasagne, biechi, blécs
Emilia Romagna	Bassetti, garganelli, lasagne, malfattini, pappardelle, pisarei, pistadein, sciufuloti, strichetti, stringotti, tagliatelle, taglierini
Tuscany	Pappardelle, pici or pinci, macaroni, pannicelli, strapponi, tacconi, gnudi
Umbria	Blò-blò, ciriole, strascinati, stringozzi, umbricelli
Marche	Cresc' tajat, lumachelle, maccheroncini, pappardelle, pataluc, pezzòle, pincinelle, tacconi, taglierini, tajuli
Lazio	Cecapreti, celliti, ciacamarini, ciufulitti, curiole, fettuccine, fregnacce, jaccoli o maccheroni (macaroni) a fezze, lombrichelli, pencarelli, ramiccia, sagne, sfusellati, tonnarelli
Abruzzo and Molise	Cavatelli, chitarrine, ciufolitti, fregnacce, fusilli, laganelle, maccheroni alla chitarra and al rintrocilo, papicci, scrippelle, tacconcelle, taccozzelle, tagliolini, tajarille, volanelle, zengarielle
Campania	Cecatielli, fusilli, lagane, maccaronara, pettole, schiaffoni, scialiatielli, strangulaprevete, triili
Apulia	Cajuddi, capunti, cavatelli, cicatielli, lagane, laganelle, mignuic, orecchiette, pociacche or pestazzule, stacchioddi, strascinati, trie, troccoli

Basilicata	Cavatelli, fusilli, lagane, manatelle, minnich or maccheroni (macaroni) col ferro, orecchiette, sagne 'ncannulate, scialatielli
Calabria	Cannaruozzoli o canneroni, ferrazzuoli, filatelli or filatieddi, lagane, maccaruni di casa, nocchetedde, sagne, rascatieddi o ricchielle, scivateddi o scilatelli, strangolapreti
Sicilia	Cavatiddi, cruselli o rosette, busiati or pasta busiata, gnoccoli, lasagna, maccaruneddi, tagghiarinas
Sardegna	Ciciones, fregula, malloreddus, maccarrones (macaroni) a ferritus o de busa, marraconese de patata, pillas or pillus

Weights and Measures

	METRIC
1 teaspoon = 60 drops	
water, milk, oil, etc.	1/6 fl oz - 5 ml
flour, salt, sugar (level)	1/6 oz - 5 g
flour, salt, sugar (heaping)	1/3 oz -10 g
1 tablespoon = 3 teaspoons	
water, milk, oil, etc	1/2 fl oz - 15 ml
flour, salt, sugar (level)	1/2 oz - 15 g
flour, salt, sugar, rice (heaping)	1 oz - 30 g
grated cheese (heaping)	1/2 oz - 15 g
butter	1/2 oz - 15 g
1 cup = 16 tablespoons	
water, milk, oil, etc	8 fl oz - 230 ml
flour	5 oz - 140 g
sugar, rice	7 oz - 200 g
1 glass	
water glass	3/4 cup – 7 fl oz - 200 ml
wine glass	1/2 cup – 4 fl oz - 120 ml
liqueur glass	1/4 cup – 2 fl oz - 60 ml

Basic Italian Cooking Sauces

Ragù bolognese

Bolognese ragu

Serves 6

- 5 ounces ground beef
- 5 ounces ground pork
- 3 ounces pancetta, minced
- 1 carrot, peeled and diced
- 1 stalk celery, diced
- 1 onion, diced
- 8 ounces peeled ripe tomatoes, seeds removed, chopped
- 1 tablespoon tomato paste
- 3 tablespoons butter
- ½ cup red wine
- 1 cup broth
- ½ cup heavy cream (optional)
- olive oil
- salt and pepper

1. In a deep skillet, warm the butter with 3 tablespoons of olive oil. Add the pancetta, onion, carrot and celery and sauté over low heat for about 1 minutes.

2. When the vegetables start to brown, add the pork and beef. Season with salt and pepper and cook, stirring for a couple of minutes. Deglaze with the wine and cook until it evaporates.

3. Add the peeled tomatoes and continue to cook, covered for 30 minutes. At this point, stir in the tomato paste diluted in ½ cup of warm water or stock. Continue to cook over low heat, covered for about 1 hour. At the end, before removing from the heat, add the heavy cream and cook until it starts to reduce.

RAGÙ NAPOLETANO O "RRAÙ DEL GUARDAPORTA"

Neapolitan or Doorkeeper's ragu

Serves 6

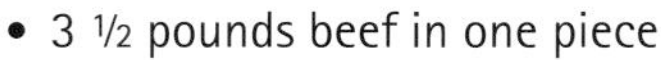

- 3 1/2 pounds beef in one piece
- 2 ounces prosciutto crudo
- 4 ounces pancetta
- 2 large onions
- 2 cloves garlic
- 1/2 cup dry red wine
- 2 tablespoons tomato paste
- 14 ounces peeled ripe tomatoes, seeds removed and chopped
- olive oil
- salt and freshly ground pepper

1. Chop the prosciutto into strips and roll it in pepper. Lard the beef with the prosciutto and set aside. In a skillet over medium heat, warm the olive oil. Add the pancetta, onion and garlic and sauté until soft. Add the meat and brown on all sides. Cover and cook slowly, turning occasionally.
2. When the onion starts to brown, deglaze with half the wine and cook until it starts to evaporate. Add the remaining wine and cook slowly, covered, for about 1 hour, or until it starts to become thick.
3. At this point, add the tomatoes and the tomato paste dissolved in enough boiling water to cover the beef. Season with salt and bring to a boil. Lower the heat and simmer for 3 hours.
4. Remove the meat from the skillet and keep warm. Cook the sauce for another hour, or until reduced by half. Slice the meat and serve with the sauce.

SUGO DI CARNE TOSCANO

Tuscan ragu

Serves 6

- 14 ounces beef (rump steak, brisket), sliced
- 14 ounces peeled ripe tomatoes, seeds removed and chopped
- 2 cups combined chopped celery, onion and carrot
- 6 tablespoons olive oil
- salt and freshly ground pepper

1. In a skillet over medium heat, warm the olive oil. Add the parsley, celery, onion and carrot and cook for 20 minutes. Add the slices of meat and brown on both sides.
2. Remove the meat from the skillet and chop finely. Return to the skillet and add the tomatoes. Season with salt and pepper and cook slowly, covered, for about 1 hour.

RAGÙ PUGLIESE O "DEL MACELLAIO"

Apulian or Butcher's ragu

Serves 8

- 5 ounces beef, cubed
- 5 ounces pork, cubed
- 5 ounces lamb, cubed
- 4 ounces pancetta, diced
- 9 ounces peeled ripe tomatoes, seeds removed and chopped
- 1 tablespoon tomato paste
- 1 onion, chopped
- 2 cloves garlic, minced
- ½ cup dry white wine
- minced chili pepper to taste
- 6 tablespoons olive oil
- salt

1. In a deep skillet, warm the olive oil. Add the onion, garlic and chili pepper and cook until they start to brown.
2. Add the pancetta and cook until browned. Deglaze with half the wine and cook until it starts to evaporate. Add the lamb, beef and pork, deglaze with the remaining wine and cook until it starts to evaporate.
3. Add the tomatoes and the tomato paste, season with salt and pepper and cook over low heat, covered, for about 2 hours, adding hot water if it starts to dry.
Add chopped chicken or sausage the last 30 minutes of the cooking time if desired.

Ragù di rigaglie

Giblets ragu

Serves 6

- 9 ounces chicken innards (liver, heart, gizzard)
- 9 ounces peeled ripe tomatoes, seeds removed and chopped
- 1 medium onion
- 2 sage leaves
- 1/2 cup wine
- 2 tablespoons butter
- 3 tablespoons olive oil
- salt and freshly ground pepper

1. Trim and chop the chicken innards. In a skillet over medium heat, melt the butter with the oil. Add the onion and sage and sauté until soft.
2. Add the gizzard, cook for about 2 minutes and deglaze with the wine. When it begins to evaporate, add the tomatoes, season with salt and pepper and cook until it thickens.
3. At this point, add the liver and heart. Cook for another 10 minutes and remove from the heat.

Ragù bianco

White ragu

Serves 6

- 6 ounces veal
- 5 ounces pork
- 4 ounces chicken breast
- 1 small onion, chopped
- 1 small carrot, peeled and diced
- rosemary
- 1/2 cup white wine
- stock
- 4 tablespoons olive oil
- salt and freshly ground pepper

1. In a skillet, warm the olive oil. Add the carrot, onion and rosemary.
2. When the onion starts to soften, add the meat. Deglaze with the wine and cook until it evaporates.
3. Remove the meat from the skillet and chop finely. Return to the skillet and season with salt and pepper. Cook for another 30 minutes, adding stock gradually.
4. Cook until the sauce starts to thicken. The sauce should be homogenous and creamy enough to serve over fettuccine or tagliatelle (noodles).

Salsa di funghi

Mushroom sauce

Serves 6

- 10 ounces fresh porcini mushrooms
- 10 ounces peeled ripe tomatoes, seeds removed, chopped
- 2 cloves garlic
- chopped mint or parsley
- 6 tablespoons olive oil
- salt and freshly ground pepper

1. Wash and peel the mushrooms and chop. In a skillet over medium heat, warm the olive oil. Add the garlic and herbs and when they start to brown, add the mushrooms.
2. Season with salt and pepper and cook, stirring with a wooden spoon, until the liquid starts to evaporate. Add the tomatoes (if you want to make a white sauce, add vegetable stock instead) and continue to cook for 20 minutes.

SUGO D'ARROSTO O "SUGO DI CARNE" O "FONDO BRUNO"

Roast sauce or "Gravy"

Serves 4

- 1 pound beef or veal pieces
- 1/4 cup plus 1 1/2 tablespoons butter
- 4 tablespoons olive oil
- 1 onion, finely chopped
- 1 stalk celery, finely chopped
- 1 carrot, finely chopped
- 1 teaspoon tomato paste
- 1 whole clove
- meat broth (liquid or bouillon cube)
- 1 teaspoon flour

1. Sauté the meat in 1/4 cup butter and the olive oil over high heat until the meat begins to brown. Add the onion, celery, carrot, tomato paste and clove.
2. Cook slowly for about 2 hours or longer, moistening occasionally with meat broth.
3. Remove the meat and eliminate almost all of the fat and all of the vegetables and the clove from the sauce by filtering it through a fine strainer. Add the flour (or cornstarch or similar starch) and remaining butter along with some more broth until a very smooth sauce is obtained.

This sauce is ideal tossed with Piedmontese agnolotti and tajarin (very thin taglierini).

SALSA DI POMODORO O "PUMMAROLA"

Traditional tomato sauce

Serves 8

- 2 pounds peeled ripe tomatoes, seeds removed and chopped
- 1 medium onion, finely chopped
- 1 stalk celery, chopped
- 2 carrots, peeled and diced
- 6 basil leaves, shredded
- 8 tablespoons olive oil
- chopped parsley
- salt

1. In a large skillet, combine the olive oil with the tomatoes, onion, celery, carrot, basil and parsley.
2. Season with salt and place over medium heat. Cook for about 1 hour.
3. Set aside to cool and strain into a food mill.
4. Return the strained sauce to the stove and cook to the desired consistency.

SUGO "FINTO" O "SCAPPATO" O "DI POMODORO"

"False" tomato ragu

Serves 4

- 1 pound peeled tomatoes, seeds removed, chopped
- 1 medium onion, finely chopped
- 2 medium carrots, peeled and diced
- 2 stalks celery, diced
- chopped parsley
- ½ cup red wine
- olive oil
- salt and freshly ground pepper

1. In a skillet over medium heat, warm 6 tablespoons of olive oil. Add the carrot, onion and celery and sauté.
2. When the vegetables are soft, add the parsley and deglaze with the wine. Cook over low heat until the wine starts to evaporate.
3. Add the tomatoes, season with salt and pepper and cook for about 1 hour, stirring occasionally. The sauce should be thick and flavorful.

BÉCHAMEL SAUCE

Serves 4 (makes about 2 cups)

- 1/4 cup butter
- 3 1/2 tablespoons flour
- 1 cup milk, heated to just below boiling point
- salt and pepper
- ground nutmeg

1. In a small saucepan, melt the butter. Add the flour and cook, continually stirring, for a few minutes.
2. Continue to stir while slowly adding the boiled milk, a little at time.
3. Lightly season with salt and pepper and a little nutmeg. Continue to cook slowly, continually stirring, for about 10 more minutes.

The ingredient amounts in this recipe are for a béchamel sauce with just the right consistency. Therefore, if for certain purposes, you need a sauce with a more liquid consistency, decrease the amount of flour and butter or increase the amount of milk according to your needs.

Recipes

Identifyng the recipes

The recipes identified with a **green-colored** title are based on a **vegetable or cheese**, the ones in **blue** contain **fish and seafood**, and the **red** ones are based on **meat or meat products.**

Ingredient Notes

Before trying the recipes, I strongly recommend reading these brief ingredient notes that contain important information for successfully making them.

Garlic and Red Hot Pepper • In sauces, fresh garlic is unsurpassed, but nowadays you can replace it with garlic paste or powder (1 medium fresh garlic clove equals 1 teaspoon paste and 1/8 teaspoon powder). In many recipes, garlic that has been preminced can also be used (1 medium fresh garlic clove equals 1/4 teaspoon minced). The same goes for hot red pepper, available in flakes, which is commonly used in recipes, as well as powder (sold as ground red pepper or cayenne pepper).

Battuto • A battuto is an Italian culinary term that refers to a finely chopped mixture of vegetables and/or herbs that provide a flavor base for a recipe. An excellent and classic battuto contains onion, celery and carrot, and has an unbeatable aroma. In the absence of fresh vegetables or to save time, frozen chopped ones can be used. In the recipes in this book, the appropriate battuto ingredients and amounts have been listed for you.

Broth • Apart from the classic broth for soups (which must be done with all the right ingredients), for most recipes, when you have to use "a little broth," it's good to use broth powder or vegetable bouillon cubes. There are exceptions, however, such as the broth for tortellini, anolini, etc. In this case, it's best to use beef or capon broth, according to different local traditions (*brodo in terza, tre brodi, etc.*).

Cheese • Some of the cheeses are written with capital letters and others with lowercase. Cheeses with capitals are those that are protected cheeses, known as DOP (Protected Designation of Origin). These include cheeses such as **Parmigiano-Reggiano** (DOP parmesan) and **Pecorino Romano** (a hard DOP sheep's milk cheese). For other cheese varieties, if possible, try to use the DOP or high-quality brand of cheese from its proper region. For example, for mozzarella, it's best to use **Mozzarella di Bufala Campana** (buffalo mozzarella). When shopping, it's helpful to look for the DOP or another mark of indication.

Olive Oil • In the recipes, the term "olive oil" is written, because for me, olive oil is simply the oil extracted from olives, but since the labeling of olive oil is another thing, then use only the "extra-virgin" kind. Where possible, I always prefer to use the olive oil produced in the region where the recipe is from: for example to make Genovese pesto, I use a delicate extra virgin olive oil from the Ligurian Riviera; for the orecchiette with broccoli rabe recipe, I instead prefer to use a delicious virgin olive oil from Apulia; and with Tuscan bean soup, a fruity olive oil from this region is best.

Cream • I am against using cream in pasta, however, in some rare cases, you can use a little of it; but you must only use **heavy cream**, which is fresh and light with a liquid consistency and is easy to whip. Never use what is known as "light cream" (it has a long shelf life), which is as thick as glue and masks flavors.

Tomatoes • In many of the recipes that require the use of fresh, ripe tomatoes, the possibility of using canned tomatoes (including liquid) is also noted. Canned peeled tomatoes are convenient and still taste good, but never use ready-made tomato puree or prepared tomato sauces. If you would like to use fresh ripe tomatoes, remember that 2 cups canned peeled tomatoes is equivalent to about 2 large fresh tomatoes.

Wine • White wine, and more rarely red wine, is added to sauces and cooked until it has reduced. You can use any wine, even the boxed kind, providing that it's not spoiled or vinegary.

Bigoli con l'Anatra o "Bìgoi co l'arna"

Bigoli with Duck

Serves 4

- 1 onion, finely chopped
- 1 stalk celery, finely chopped
- 1 carrot, finely chopped
- 1 whole clove
- 1 bay leaf
- salt
- 1 young duck, about 3 pounds (with giblets), cleaned
- 3 sage leaves
- ½ cup butter
- pepper
- 1 pound bigoli al torchio (see note) or thick spaghetti
- grated Parmigiano-Reggiano

1 Fill a pot with 8 cups water. Add the onion, celery, carrot, clove and bay leaf to the pot and season with salt. Bring the pot to a boil, then add the duck, together with its giblets. Cook slowly for at least an hour, removing any foam and impurities.

2 Remove the duck from the broth and, with a slotted spoon, remove all of the vegetables and giblets. Reserve the broth and set aside.

3 Chop the giblets (heart, liver and gizzard) and, in a saucepan, sauté them along with the boiled vegetables and sage in the butter. Season with salt and pepper and cook over high heat for about 10 minutes.

4 Filter the duck broth and cook the bigoli in it, then drain and toss with the giblet sauce. Serve with the Parmigiano at the table. The boiled duck can be served as a main course with boiled potatoes and Savoy cabbage.

Bigoli is a fresh pasta, typical of the Veneto region, particularly the Bassano del Grappa area. Today it can be found in ready-made packages.

Bigoli con le Sardelle o "Bìgoi co àole de lago"

Bigoli with fresh water Sardines

Serves 4

- ½ pound salt-cured anchovies
- 1 clove garlic
- salt and pepper
- 6 tablespoons olive oil
- 1 pound bigoli al torchio or thick spaghetti
- parsley, minced
- toasted breadcrumbs (optional)

1 Remove the anchovies from the salt, clean well and fillet. Add the sardine meat and the garlic (whole) to a skillet.

2 Season with salt and pepper and add the olive oil and 3 tablespoons water. Cook over low heat for about 10 minutes, stirring and breaking up the fish meat with a wooden spoon.

3 Cook the pasta in a large pot of boiling salted water until al dente, then drain. Add the pasta to the skillet and toss well to coat. Serve with minced parsley and, if desired, sprinkled with a small amount of toasted breadcrumbs.

Fettuccine al *Triplo burro*

Triple Butter Fettuccine

Serves 4

- 1 pound fresh fettuccine or tagliatelle
- salt
- 2/3 cup butter
- pepper
- grated Pecorino Romano or Parmigiano-Reggiano or both

1 Cook the pasta in a large pot of boiling salted water until al dente, then drain. Place in a warmed serving bowl, add 3 1/2 tablespoons of the butter and stir well.

2 Once the butter has been completely absorbed, moisten with a couple of tablespoons of the pasta cooking water. Add another 3 1/2 tablespoons of butter and stir until well mixed.

3 Add the remaining butter and more pasta cooking water so that there is a good amount of butter. Stir well and serve immediately with pepper and plenty of grated cheese at the table.

Incorporating the butter three different times is not pointless: if you put the butter in all together the flavor will be different because the pasta won't absorb the fat.
Roman fettuccine are tagliatelle (sometimes with less egg in respect to the Emilian kind) that are 1/3 inch wide.
"**Fettuccine with ricotta**" is also very good; it consists of fettuccine, about 1/8 inch wide, simply dressed with very fresh ricotta romana passed through a sieve and combined with pepper and a little pasta cooking water.
There's also the lesser known "**Fettuccine alla papalina**" (Papal fettuccine); once it's been cooked until al dente, it's bathed in beaten eggs with cheese and then dressed with a sauce of onions roasted in butter, small blanched peas and cubed prosciutto cotto (cooked ham).

Frègula con le Arselle

Fregula with Clams

Serves 4

- 1 1/3 pounds arselle (small wedge shell clams) or substitute other small clams, cleaned
- 2 cloves garlic
- 6 tablespoons olive oil
- 2 tablespoons tomato puree or 14 ounces canned peeled tomatoes, chopped
- salt and pepper
- 1/4 pound medium grained Sardinian fregula (see note) or couscous (large-grain)
- 2 tablespoons parsley, minced

1 Open the clams and drain, reserving the water, and remove the meat from the shells.

2 In a pot, sauté the garlic (whole) in the olive oil. Before the garlic turns golden, add the tomato puree or peeled tomatoes and 5 1/4 cups boiling water.

3 Season with salt and pepper and bring to a boil for about 30 minutes. Add the pasta and cook for about 20 minutes.

4 Add the clams with their water and the parsley. Cook for 5 minutes and remove from the heat. Serve warm.

This delicious Sardinian dish is made with "**fregula**" a typical pasta made with coarse grain durum wheat semolina flour, mixed with warm water that has a pinch of saffron dissolved in it. The dough is rubbed with the hands to make large grains that are then dried on a dishcloth. Today they can also be found ready-made in stores. Usually they are eaten in broth, with "**casu de fitta**" (fresh pecorino) and sprinkled with grated pecorino.

Garganelli al Ragù di salsiccia

Fresh Penne rigate with Sausage Ragu

Serves 4

- 1/2 onion, finely minced
- 1 bay leaf
- 1/3 cup butter
- 1/2 pound sausage, casings removed and crumbled
- salt and pepper
- 1/2 cup white wine
- 1 pound fresh garganelli or penne rigate
- grated Parmigiano-Reggiano or pecorino

1 In a skillet, slowly sauté the onion and bay leaf in the butter. Before the onion begins to take color, add the sausage.

2 Continue to cook slowly for a few minutes, then season with salt and pepper. Add the wine and cook until it's completely reduced.

3 Cook the pasta in a large pot of boiling salted water until al dente, then drain. Immediately add to the skillet and toss well with the sauce. Moisten with a couple of tablespoons of the pasta cooking water, if needed. Serve with plenty of cheese at the table.

This sauce can also be prepared with around 2/3 pound ripe tomatoes that have been peeled and seeded.

Garganelli alle Rigaglie o "Garganèl"

Fresh Penne rigate with Giblets sauce

Serves 6 - 8

- pasta dough made from 4 cups flour and 5 eggs
- 1 onion, chopped
- 3 sage leaves
- 1/4 cup butter
- 2/3 pound chicken livers and hearts, cleaned and chopped
- 1/2 cup white wine
- 2 ripe tomatoes, peeled and chopped or 2 cups peeled canned tomatoes, chopped
- salt and pepper
- grated Parmigiano-Reggiano

1 Prepare the dough and roll it out, not too thin, and cut it into squares about 2 inches in diameter. Starting from a corner, roll up each square on a stick and roll them over a garganelli "comb" so that they are like horizontal "penne rigate." Let them dry for a few hours on a floured surface.

2 In a skillet, sauté the onion and sage in the butter until the onion is almost softened. Add the chicken livers and heart and the wine and let it reduce.

3 Add the tomatoes and season with salt and pepper. Cook until the sauce has thickened.

4 Cook the pasta in a large pot of boiling salted water until al dente, then drain. Place in a warmed serving bowl and toss with the sauce and plenty of Parmigiano.

Garganelli can also be cooked **in broth**. In this case, you add 3 tablespoons of Parmigiano and nutmeg essence to the dough. Another traditional recipe is "**garganelli with vegetables**." Prepare a sauce by sautéing 4 ounces of diced prosciutto cotto (cooked ham) in 1/3 cup butter, then adding 2/3 cup of barley parboiled peas and 2 diced sweet red peppers. When it's almost cooked, add 1/4 cup cream or milk and continue to cook for about 10 more minutes.

Giuget

Small Lasagna Romagna-style

Serves 6

- 2 1/2 cups all-purpose flour
- 1 1/4 cups yellow cornmeal
- 2 eggs
- salt
- 2 onions
- 1 stalk celery
- 1 carrot
- 1/3 cup butter
- 3 sausages, casings removed and crumbled
- 4 ounces pancetta, cubed
- 1/2 cup white wine
- pepper
- grated Parmigiano-Reggiano

1 Mix the two flours together well. Prepare a pasta dough with the flour mixture, the eggs, warm water and salt. Roll out, not too thin, and cut it into squares, about 1 1/2 inches in diameter.

2 In a saucepan, sauté the onions, carrot and celery in the butter until they're just softened. Add the sausage, pancetta and wine and cook until the wine reduces.

3 Season with salt and pepper and cook for about 30 minutes, adding water or broth.

4 Cook the pasta in a large pot of boiling salted water until al dente, then drain. Place in a warmed serving bowl and toss with the sauce and some Parmigiano.

Lasagne Bastarde o "Armelette"

Mixed flour Lasagna

Serves 6 -8

- 3 1/4 cups all-purpose flour
- 1 2/3 cups chestnut flour
- 4 eggs
- salt
- 1 cup sheep's milk ricotta
- 3 tablespoons grated Parmigiano-Reggiano, plus extra
- 3 tablespoons grated pecorino, plus extra
- freshly ground black pepper

1 Sift and mix the flours well together. Mound the flour mixture and add the eggs, a pinch of salt and a little cold water to the center. Work together to form the dough and set aside to rest wrapped in plastic in the refrigerator for 1 hour.

2 Roll out to a thin sheet and cut into squares or diamonds, about 3 inches across (tagliatelle or pappardelle are also excellent).

3 Cook for a few minutes in a large pot of boiling salted water. Meanwhile, in a warmed serving bowl, mix the ricotta with 3 tablespoons of the pasta cooking water, the Parmigiano and pecorino. Drain with a slotted spoon and place in the serving bowl.

4 Serve sprinkled with more cheese and freshly ground black pepper.

This excellent pasta is widespread in Lunigiana and Garfagnana, and can be topped with a classic Genovese pesto or simply with olive oil and grated cheese (Parmigiano or pecorino).

Lasagne alla Bolognese

Lasagna Bolognese

Serves 6

- Green pasta dough made from 4 cups flour, 3 eggs and 1 cup finely chopped boiled spinach
- Salt
- 2 tablespoons olive oil
- Béchamel sauce made from 1/2 cup flour, 1/4 cup butter and 3 cups milk (see recipe)
- Bolognese sauce (see recipe)
- Grated Parmigiano-Reggiano
- 1/4 cup butter

Unfortunately many restaurants ruin superb dishes. Do not make any changes to this perfect recipe and do not use dry lasagna noodles. According to tradition, green dough should be used, but you can make the recipe with yellow lasagna (**lasagna ferrara**) or with alternating layers of yellow and green.

1 Prepare the green dough with the flour, eggs and spinach. Roll it out as thin as possible and cut into rectangles about 4 x 6 inches. Cook the lasagna noodles for a few minutes, a few at a time, in a large pot of boiling salted water with the olive oil added to it. Drain with a slotted spoon and place on a damp towel.

2 Grease a baking pan or dish, about 4 inches deep. Put some of the béchamel sauce on the bottom, followed by a layer of lasagna noodles.

3 Top with some of the meat sauce (do not completely cover the pasta), followed by a layer of béchamel and grated cheese. Continue to make the layers in this way, so that it reaches about halfway up the pan, ending with a layer of béchamel sauce, covered with dots of butter and Parmigiano.

4 Place in the oven at 350° for about 20 minutes (the surface should not be browned). Wait a few minutes before serving.

Lasagne con il Pesce

Seafood Lasagna

Serves 6 - 8

- pasta dough made from 4 cups flour and 3 eggs
- salt
- 2 tablespoons olive oil
- flour for dredging
- 1 3/4 pound fresh flatfish (sole, turbot, John Dory)
- 3/4 pound shrimp, tails intact
- 1/2 cup butter
- 2 cups béchamel sauce (see recipe)
- pepper
- grated Parmigiano-Reggiano

This delicious lasagna is an interpretation of a traditional Renaissance dish, described by Cristoforo Messisbugo in one of his books published in Ferrara in 1549. It can also be made with green lasagna or both yellow and green noodles.

1 Make a normal pasta dough with the flour, eggs and a little cold water. Roll out very thin and cut into lasagna noodles, about 4 x 6 inches in size. Cook the lasagna noodles for a few minutes, a few at a time, in a large pot of boiling salted water with the olive oil added to it. Drain with a slotted spoon, then place briefly in cold water, then on a towel to dry

2 Lightly flour the fish and shrimp. In a skillet, melt half the butter. Add the fish and shrimp and cook for 5 minutes, then moisten with a little water.

3 After 5 minutes remove from heat and set aside to cool thoroughly. Fillet the fish and shell the shrimp.

4 On the bottom of a buttered baking dish, put some of the béchamel sauce, then make a layer of lasagna noodles. Cover with a layer of fish and shrimp, followed by salt, pepper, a little butter, the seafood cooking sauce and some more béchamel sauce.

5 Continue to make the layers in this way, so that it reaches about 2 inches high, ending with a layer of béchamel sauce. Sprinkle the top with Parmigiano and place in the oven at 400° for about for about 30 minutes.

Lasagne al Pesto o "Mandilli de saèa"

Pesto Lasagna

Serves 4 - 6

- pasta dough made from 3 1/4 cups type 0 flour and 2 eggs
- 1 cup basil (about 30 leaves)
- 1/2 clove garlic
- 1 teaspoon coarse salt
- 2 tablespoons pine nuts
- 2 tablespoons grated Parmigiano-Reggiano, plus extra
- 2 tablespoons grated pecorino, plus extra
- 1/2 cup plus 1 tablespoon extra virgin olive oil

A delicious and little known recipe from Liguria, this lasagna is called "**mandilli de saèa**" meaning "silk handkerchiefs," and is very thin and delicate. In addition to pesto, it can be made with a "**touch" of meat or stew**, in other words, with a sauce made by slowly cooking a piece of beef or veal with vegetables and herbs, dried mushrooms and tomatoes. The meat is served as a main course.

1 Prepare a normal pasta dough with the flour, eggs and a little water. Roll out very thinly and make rather large lasagna squares, about 5 to 6 inches in diameter.

2 Clean the basil leaves with a cloth (without washing them) with the stems and large ribbed parts removed. Put them in a mortar and add the garlic and coarse salt. With a pestle start to crush the ingredients against the sides with a turning motion (not up and down) until the basil is well crushed. Add the pine nuts and continue to crush. (If you don't have a mortar and pestle, you can use a food processor, but the result will not be the same).

3 Put the pesto in a warmed bowl and add the Parmigiano and pecorino, mix well and add 1/2 cup olive oil in a slow, steady stream, while stirring constantly, so that you get a rather thick sauce.

4 Put a tablespoon of the pesto on the bottom of large individual bowls. Cook the pasta in a large pot of boiling salted water with 1 tablespoon olive oil added to it. Drain the pasta with a slotted spoon and place some lasagna directly in each of the bowls. Cover with more pesto, followed by two more lasagna and pesto layers. Serve immediately sprinkled with a mixture of Parmigiano and pecorino.

Maccheroncini di Campofilone al Ragù

Campofilone Macaroni with Ragu

Serves 4

- 1 onion, finely diced
- 1 carrot, finely diced
- 1 stalk celery, finely diced
- 6 tablespoons olive oil
- 1/3 pound ground veal
- 1/4 pound ground pork
- 1 chicken liver, chopped
- 1/2 cup white wine
- 2 large ripe tomatoes, peeled and chopped or 2 cups peeled canned tomatoes, chopped
- pinch of ground clove
- pinch of ground nutmeg
- salt and pepper
- 1 pound extra thin fresh egg tagliolini
- grated pecorino

1 In a saucepan, gently sauté the onion, carrot and celery in the olive oil until just softened. Add the ground meat and chicken liver and cook for a few minutes.

2 Add the wine and cook until it reduces.

3 Add the tomatoes, clove and nutmeg and season with salt and pepper.

4 Cook slowly until the meat is cooked through and the sauce has thickened.

5 Cook the pasta in boiling salted water until al dente. Toss with plenty of sauce and serve with grated cheese and more sauce at the table.

Campofilone is a village in Marche in the province of Fermo, known for its *spaghettini* that is as thin as angel hair and for its egg *maccheroncini* or *maccheroncelli*, which is also just as thin.

Maccheroni alla Contadina

Peasant-style Macaroni

Serves 4

- 4 artichokes, cleaned and coarsely chopped
- 1 small onion, coarsely chopped
- 1 sprig parsley, minced
- 2 sausages, casings removed and crumbled
- 6 tablespoons olive oil
- salt and pepper
- 1 1/2 large ripe tomatoes, peeled and chopped or 1 1/2 cups peeled canned tomatoes, chopped
- 1 pound fresh tagliatelle or pappardelle
- grated Parmigiano-Reggiano

1 In a saucepan, sauté the artichokes, onion, parsley and sausage in the olive oil until the sausage is well browned. Season with salt and pepper and cook for 5 minutes.

2 Add the tomatoes and cook over low heat for 30 more minutes.

3 ook the pasta in a large pot of boiling salted water until al dente, then drain. Place in a warmed serving bowl and toss well with the sauce. Serve hot with Parmigano-Reggiano at the table.

Maccheroni maremmani ai Fegatini

Maremma-style Macaroni with Chicken Liver Sauce

Serves 4

- 1 onion, finely diced
- 1 carrot, finely diced
- 1 stalk celery, finely diced
- 6 tablespoons olive oil
- 2 ounces pancetta
- 1/2 pound chicken livers, chopped
- 1/2 cup red wine
- salt and pepper
- 1 ounce dried mushrooms, soaked and coarsely chopped
- 1 1/2 large ripe tomatoes, peeled and chopped or 1 1/2 cups peeled canned tomatoes, chopped
- 1 pound fresh pappardelle or tagliatelle
- grated Parmigiano-Reggiano

1 In a saucepan, sauté the onion, celery and carrot in the olive oil until softened. Add the pancetta, chicken livers and red wine.

2 Season with salt and pepper and cook until it reduces. Add the mushrooms and tomatoes and cook slowly for about 30 minutes.

3 Cook the pasta in a large pot of boiling salted water until al dente, then drain. Place in a warmed serving bowl and toss with the sauce and Parmigano.

Maccheroni ai Funghi

Mushroom Macaroni

Serves 4

- 2 cloves garlic
- 6 tablespoons olive oil
- 1/2 cup white wine
- 1 large ripe tomato, peeled and chopped, or substitute 1 cup peeled canned tomatoes, chopped
- salt and pepper
- 8 ounces porcini mushrooms, cleaned and coarsely chopped
- 1/4 cup parsley, minced
- 1 pound macaroni (see note) or pappardelle
- grated Parmigiano-Reggiano (optional)

1 In a skillet, sauté the garlic (whole) in 6 tablespoons of the olive oil, until it just begins to turn golden. Add the wine and let it reduce. Add the tomatoes and season with salt and pepper. Continue to cook, removing the garlic cloves after 15 minutes. Add the mushrooms and parsley and continue to cook slowly for 15 more minutes.

2 Cook the pasta in a large pot of boiling salted water until al dente, then drain. Pour directly into the skillet with the sauce.

3 Cook for a few minutes and serve hot with Parmigiano-Reggiano at the table, if desired.

The macaroni used in this recipe is made from pasta dough squares, about 3 inches in diameter, using eggs (2 eggs per 3 1/4 cups flour), water and salt. In Lucca these are called "**tacconi**."
You can also use pappardelle, nastroni or wide tagliatelle.

Maccheroni al Ragù d'agnello

Macaroni with Lamb Ragu

Serves 4

- ½ onion, finely chopped
- 1 clove garlic, finely chopped
- 2-3 sprigs rosemary, finely chopped
- 6 tablespoons olive oil
- ⅔ pound lamb cubes
- salt and pepper
- ½ cup white wine
- 2 large ripe tomatoes, peeled and chopped or 2 cups peeled canned tomatoes, chopped
- 1 pound maccheroni al ferretto or substitute rigatoni (see note)

1 In a skillet, sauté the onion, garlic and rosemary in the olive oil, until the onion has softened.

2 Add the lamb and let it brown for a few minutes.

3 Season with salt and pepper, add the wine and let it reduce. Add the tomatoes and cook for about 1 hour, stirring frequently, and sprinkling with water or broth, as needed.

4 Cook the pasta in a large pot of boiling salted water until al dente, then drain. Place in a warmed serving bowl and toss with the lamb ragu.

Maccheroni al ferro (ironed macaroni) are made with durum wheat flour mixed with water and salt; the dough is rolled out, not too thin, and is then cut into squares, about 1½ inches in diameter. A special iron is placed on top of the squares and is moved back and forth so that the dough rolls up around the iron itself; it's then left to rest for a few hours before cooking. Today it can be found ready-made by many different pasta producers.

Maccheroni alla chitarra al Ragù d'agnello

Spaghetti alla Chitarra with Lamb Ragu

Serves 4

- flour for dredging
- 2/3 pound lamb cubes
- 2 cloves garlic
- pinch of hot red pepper flakes
- 1 bay leaf
- 6 tablespoons olive oil
- 1 cup white wine
- 1 1/2 large ripe tomatoes, peeled and chopped or 1 1/2 cups peeled canned tomatoes, chopped
- 2 red or yellow peppers, cut into strips
- salt and pepper
- 1 pound macaroni or spaghetti alla chitarra

1 Lightly flour the lamb cubes. In a skillet, sauté the garlic, hot red pepper flakes, bay leaf and floured lamb cubes in the olive oil, stirring often, until the meat is browned. Add 1/2 cup wine to the skillet and let it completely reduce. Add the remaining wine and let it reduce again.

2 Add the tomatoes and peppers and season with salt and pepper. Cook over low heat for about an hour, until the meat becomes tender.

3 Cook the pasta in a large pot of boiling salted water until al dente, then drain and toss with the lamb ragu.

Macaroni or **spaghetti alla chitarra** is a specialty of Abruzzo, made with durum wheat flour and lots of eggs. The dough is rolled out to about 1/8 inch thick, and is then placed on a special tool called a "chitarra" (guitar). The dough is laid over the strings and a rolling pin is rolled over it to create square-shaped spaghetti. All pasta producers now commonly make it in both dry and fresh versions. Apulian "**troccoli**" (see recipe) are quite similar, but are larger and oval.

Maccheroni Strappati

"Torn" Macaroni with Sausage and Veal sauce

Serves 6

- 1 onion, chopped
- 6 tablespoons olive oil
- 2 sausages, casings removed and crumbled
- 1/4 pound ground lean veal
- 1/4 pound chicken livers, chopped
- bay leaves
- nutmeg
- salt and pepper
- 2 large ripe tomatoes, peeled and chopped or 2 cups peeled canned tomatoes, chopped
- pasta dough made with 3 1/4 cups flour and 2 eggs
- grated Parmigiano-Reggiano

1 Sauté the onion in the olive oil. Add the sausages, veal and chicken livers and season with bay leaves, nutmeg, salt and pepper. Cook until the meat is browned.

2 Add the tomatoes and cook for about an hour.

3 Roll out the dough rather thin and "tear" with your hands into irregular pieces. Cook in a large pot of boiling salted water for a few minutes, then drain with a slotted spoon.

4 In a serving bowl, which has been heated with boiling water, put a layer of the sauce and a little Parmigiano. Add a layer of the pasta and continue to make the layers in this way, ending with sauce and cheese. Serve in a few minutes.

Macco di Fave e pasta

Fava Beans and Mash Tagliatelle

Serves 4

- 8 ounces dry fava beans
- 1/2 red onion, thinly sliced
- 4 ripe cherry tomatoes, peeled and seeded
- Salt and pepper
- 1/2 cup high-quality extra virgin olive oil
- 1/3 pound semolina (not egg) tagliatelle
- grated pecorino

1 Soak the beans overnight, then peel and put them in a pot with the onion, 5 1/4 cups water and the tomatoes and season with salt and pepper.

2 Cook, covered, over low heat for about an hour or more, stirring often, until the beans are soft, crushing any beans that are still whole.

3 Add the olive oil and pasta to the pot and cook until the pasta is al dente, making sure the liquid remains rather thick. Remove from the heat and set aside for a few minutes. Serve with pecorino and pepper.

Macco is a peasant soup popular in many southern regions. It is a puree of dry fava beans that comes from "puls fabata," a kind of polenta used by the Roman people. This recipe is typical of Basilicata and Calabria, but there is also a Sicilian fava "**maccu**" that is very similar, but it requires the addition of some chopped wild fennel.
The word macco comes from "*ammaccare, schiacciare*" (to squash, crush) and, in fact, the beans need to be crushed in a pot.

Malloreddus alla Campidanese

Small Sardinian Gnocchi with meat sauce

Serves 6 - 8

- 4 3/4 cups durum wheat flour or semolina flour
- 3 tablespoons olive oil
- pinch of saffron, dissolved in a little warm water
- 1/4 pound lardo, or substitute pancetta, diced
- 1 small onion, finely chopped
- 1/4 pound ground veal
- 1/4 pound ground pork
- 2 ounces sausage
- rosemary or bay leaves
- salt and pepper
- 4 large ripe tomatoes, peeled and chopped or 4 cups peeled canned tomatoes, chopped
- grated Pecorino Sardo

1 Prepare a dough with the flour, 1 tablespoon of the olive oil, salt and saffron water. Work together, adding more water if needed, until a smooth and rather firm dough is obtained. Wrap the dough in plastic wrap and let rest for 30 minutes.

2 Divide the dough into pieces and form the dough into ropes, about 1/8 inch thick. Cut each rope into pieces, about 3/4 inch wide. Using your thumb, roll the dough pieces on the bottom of a metal sieve, so that they're marked up. Let them dry on a floured surface for at least 1 day.

3 In a saucepan, sauté the lardo and onion in 2 tablespoons of the olive oil, until the onion just begins to take color. Add the ground meats, sausage and a little rosemary or bay leaves and sauté for a few minutes.

4 Season with salt and pepper and add the tomatoes. Cook slowly for about an hour, adding hot water if need.

5 Cook the pasta in a large pot of boiling salted water until al dente. Toss with the sauce and plenty of Pecorino Sardo.

Malmaritati alla Bolognese

Short Tagliatelle with Bean Soup

Serves 6

- 8 ounces dry borlotti (cranberry) beans
- ½ onion, finely chopped
- 2 cloves garlic, finely chopped
- 2 ounces lardo, or substitute pancetta, diced
- 4 tablespoons olive oil
- 2 tablespoons parsley, finely chopped
- 1 large ripe tomato, peeled and chopped or 1 cup peeled canned tomatoes, chopped
- salt and pepper
- ¾ pound maltagliati or squares of fresh pasta (see note)
- grated Parmigiano-Reggiano

1 Soak the beans overnight in 10 cups cold water, then boil in a large pot of water. Remove from the heat and set aside to cool in the pot. Mash half of the beans using a food mill or food processor and transfer them back to the cooking water.

2 In a deep skillet, sauté the onion and garlic in the lardo and olive oil until the onion begins to soften. Add the parsley and tomatoes and season with salt and pepper

3 Add the beans with all their liquid and continue to cook until just boiling. Add the pasta and cook until al dente. Serve with pepper and Parmigiano at the table.

Maltagliati are normal tagliatelle made from pasta dough that is about ½ inch wide, cut into diamonds or irregular shapes. In practice, while the dough is still rolled up, it's cut with a knife, making a straight cut and a diagonal one to form long triangles.

Inox

Maltagliati al Radicchio

Fresh Pasta with Radicchio sauce

Serves 4

- pasta dough made from 3 1/4 cups flour and 4 eggs
- 1/2 onion, finely chopped
- 6 tablespoons olive oil
- 10 ounces Treviso red radicchio, or substitute other red radicchio variety, cored and cut into strips
- 1 1/2 large ripe tomatoes, peeled and chopped or 1 1/2 cups peeled canned tomatoes, chopped
- salt and pepper
- grated Parmigiano-Reggiano

1 Prepare a normal pasta dough and roll it out thin. Using a knife, make a straight cut and a diagonal one to form long triangles, about 1/3 inch wide.

2 In skillet, sauté the onion in the olive oil until golden brown.

3 Add the radicchio and cook for 5 minutes. Add the tomatoes, season with salt and pepper and cook over high heat for about 15 minutes.

4 Cook the pasta in a large pot of boiling salted water until al dente, then drain. Place in a warmed serving bowl and toss with the radicchio sauce. Serve with Parmigiano at the table.

Instead of maltagliati you can use fresh **macaroni** or **lasagna** dough, and cut it using a pasta wheel or knife, to form rectangles, about 1 x 2 inches in size, or squares; the shape is not very important.

Orecchiette con le Braciolette o "brasciole"

Orecchiette with Veal Cutlets

Serves 4

- 8 small slices (about 1 pound) quality veal or beef
- 8 slices pancetta
- 8 slices pecorino
- 2 cloves garlic, minced
- Parsley, minced
- salt and pepper
- 1 onion, finely diced
- 1 carrot, finely diced
- 1 stalk celery, finely diced
- 6 tablespoons olive oil
- 2 large ripe tomatoes, peeled and chopped or 2 cups peeled canned tomatoes, chopped
- 1 pound orecchiette
- grated pecorino or ricotta salata

1 Pound the meat slices thin. On top of each piece of meat place one slice each of the pancetta and pecorino and a little garlic and parsley. Season with salt and pepper and roll up each, securing with a toothpick.

2 In a saucepan, sauté the onion, celery and carrot in the olive oil until softened. Add the tomatoes and cook for 15 more minutes.

3 Add the veal rolls and cook for about an hour, until they become tender.

4 Cook the pasta in a large pot of boiling salted water until al dente, then drain. Toss with the sauce and plenty of pecorino. In the past, the veal rolls were eaten as a main course, but now they are also served along with the pasta.

Orecchiette con i Broccoli

Orecchiette with Broccoli

Serves 4

- 1 pound orecchiette
- 1 clove garlic
- 1/4 teaspoon hot red pepper flakes
- 1 anchovy, packed in salt and rinsed
- 6 tablespoons olive oil, plus extra
- 1 large bunch Italian broccoli, about 1 1/2 pounds, stems removed and cut into bite-sized pieces
- grated pecorino or cacioricotta
- salt

1 Cook the pasta in a large pot of boiling salted water until al dente. Meanwhile, in a skillet, sauté the garlic (whole), hot red pepper flakes and anchovy in the olive oil, turning and letting the anchovy dissolve in the oil.

2 Sauté the broccoli, then moisten with a little of the pasta cooking water and let simmer for 10 minutes.

3 Drain the pasta, reserving some of the cooking water, and toss in the skillet. Drizzle with a little olive oil, adding some of the pasta cooking water, if needed. Serve with the cheese.

If you want to use broccoli rabe, you can add a dozen cherry tomatoes. You can also add 1 pound clams, just opened in a skillet over high heat.

Orecchiette o "strascinate" con le Cime di rapa

Orecchiette with Broccoli Rabe

Serves 4

- 1 1/2 pounds broccoli rabe or turnip greens
- salt
- 1 pound orecchiette
- 2 cloves garlic
- 1/4 teaspoon hot red pepper flakes
- 2 anchovies, packed in salt and rinsed
- 6 tablespoons olive oil, plus extra
- grated pecorino or cacioricotta

1 Clean the broccoli rabe, leaving the most tender leaves and stems intact. Add to 1 gallon of boiling salted water along with the pasta and cook slowly, until the pasta is al dente, about 20 minutes.

2 Meanwhile, in a skillet, sauté the garlic (whole), hot red pepper flakes and anchovy in the olive oil. Stir, letting the anchovy dissolve in the hot oil.

3 Drain the pasta and broccoli rabe and toss briefly in the skillet. Serve drizzled with a little raw olive oil and sprinkled with some pecorino or fresh cacioricotta.

Traditionally, orecchiette with broccoli rabe is tossed with only raw Apulian olive oil and pepper. In addition to broccoli rabe, the orecchiette can be cooked with "**cime di cola**" (**Apulian green cauliflower**). Orecchiette can be made in slightly different shapes and sizes and is also known by different names depending on the area: **cicatielli** (Foggia), **chiangarelle** (Taranto), **stacchiodde** (Brindisi) and **recchietedde** or **strascenate** (Bari) as well as **cavatielli** or **cavatieddi**, **pociacche** and **pestazzuole**.

Orecchiette con la Rucola

Orecchiette with Arugula

Serves 4

- 2 cloves garlic
- 3 tablespoons parsley, minced
- 1/4 teaspoon hot red pepper flakes
- 6 tablespoons olive oil, plus extra
- 6 large ripe plum tomatoes, peeled, chopped and seeds removed
- salt
- 15 ounces arugula, coarsely chopped
- 1 pound orecchiette
- 1/4 cup grated pecorino, plus extra

1 In a saucepan, sauté the garlic (whole), parsley and hot red pepper flakes in the olive oil.

2 Before the garlic turns golden, add the tomatoes. Season with salt and cook for 15 minutes.

3 Cook the arugula for 5 minutes in a large pot of boiling salted water, then add the pasta to the same pot.

4 Cook the pasta until al dente, then drain along with the arugula and place in a warm serving bowl.

5 Drizzle with a little olive oil and sprinkle with the pecorino. Mix well and toss with the tomato sauce. Serve immediately with extra cheese at the table.

To make orecchiette at home, mix durum wheat semolina flour with water and a little salt and form a compact dough, then knead into small cylinders about 1/3 inch in diameter. Tear the dough into small pieces and crush them using your thumb or the tip of a knife, "dragging" them on a cutting board or floured pastry board to obtain small shells, about 3/4 to 1 inch in size.

Paglia e fieno con Piselli e prosciutto

"Straw and Hay" with Peas and Prosciutto

Serves 4

- 1/2 pound egg tagliatelline
- 1/2 pound spinach egg tagliatelline
- 1 1/3 cups shelled peas
- salt
- 1 clove garlic
- 1/3 cup butter
- pepper
- 4 ounces prosciutto cotto (cooked ham), cut into strips
- grated Parmigiano-Reggiano

1 Buy ready-made pasta or prepare your own according to the book's chapter on pasta. Cook the peas in boiling salted water for about 15 minutes, then drain.

2 In a large skillet, slowly sauté the peas with the garlic (whole) in the butter for about 10 minutes. Season with salt and pepper and add the prosciutto. Cook for a couple more minutes, then turn off the heat.

3 Cook the pasta in a large pot of boiling salted water until al dente, then drain. Add to the skillet and toss well. Add some of the pasta cooking water (or heavy cream or milk) if it's too dry. Serve immediately with cheese and freshly ground pepper at the table.

Instead of peas you can use mushrooms (cultivated) cut into thin slices and sautéed in butter. The traditional recipe uses fat and lean prosciutto crudo cut into strips.

Pappardelle con l'Anatra

Pappardelle with Duck sauce

Serves 4

- 1 onion, finely chopped
- 1 stalk celery, finely chopped
- 1 carrot, finely chopped
- 2 ounces pancetta, finely chopped
- 4 tablespoons olive oil
- ½ small duck (with liver and heart), cleaned and cut into large pieces
- 1 cup white wine
- 2 large ripe tomatoes, peeled and chopped or 2 cups peeled canned tomatoes, chopped
- salt and pepper
- ½ teaspoon crushed fennel seeds (optional)
- 1 pound fresh pappardelle or tagliatelle
- grated Parmigiano-Reggiano

1 In a saucepan, sauté the onion, celery, carrot and pancetta in the olive oil. Before the vegetables soften, add the duck and cook for 10 minutes.

2 Add the wine and let it completely reduce. Add the tomatoes, season with salt and pepper and add the fennel seeds, if desired. Cook slowly for about 30 minutes.

3 Remove the duck and eliminate as much fat from the sauce as possible. Remove the meat from the bones and shred along with the liver and heart, then add back to the sauce.

4 Cook the pasta in a large pot of boiling salted water until al dente, then drain. Place in a warmed serving bowl and toss well with the sauce. Serve sprinkled with Parmigiano. The duck can be served separately as a main course.

Pappardelle al Coniglio

Pappardelle with Rabbit sauce

Serves 4

- 1 onion, finely chopped
- 1 stalk celery, finely chopped
- 1 carrot, finely chopped
- 1 clove garlic, finely chopped
- 1 sprig rosemary, finely chopped
- 6 tablespoons olive oil
- 1/2 small rabbit, cut into pieces
- 1/2 cup white wine
- salt and pepper
- 2 large ripe tomatoes, peeled and chopped or 2 cups peeled canned tomatoes, chopped
- 1 pound fresh pappardelle or tagliatelle
- grated Parmigiano-Reggiano

1 In a saucepan, sauté the onion, celery, carrot, garlic and rosemary in the olive oil until the onion softens. Add the rabbit and cook for 10 minutes.

2 Add the wine, season with salt and pepper and cook until it reduces. Add the tomatoes and cook, covered, for about 30 minutes.

3 Remove the rabbit, then remove the meat from the bones and shred. Place the rabbit back in the saucepan and cook for 15 more minutes.

4 Cook the pasta in a large pot of boiling salted water until al dente, then drain. Place in a warmed serving bowl and toss well with the sauce. Serve with Parmigiano at the table.

In the past, this traditional peasant dish was prepared as a normal hunter-style rabbit, which was served in the sauce, without the homemade pappardelle or tagliatelle.

Pappardelle al Cinghiale

Serves 6 - 8

For the marinade:

- 2 cups red wine
- ½ cup red wine vinegar
- salt
- 2-3 bay leaves or rosemary sprigs
- 1 onion, 1 stalk celery, 1 carrot, 1 clove garlic, finely chopped

For the pappardelle:

- 1 pound wild boar, cubed
- ½ cup olive oil
- salt and pepper
- 2 large ripe tomatoes, peeled and chopped or 2 cups peeled canned tomatoes, chopped
- broth
- 1 pound fresh pappardelle
- grated Parmigiano-Reggiano or pecorino

Pappardelle with Wild Boar sauce

1 In a saucepan, sauté the onion, celery, carrot, garlic and rosemary in the olive oil until the onion softens. Add the rabbit and cook for 10 minutes.

2 Add the wine, season with salt and pepper and cook until it reduces. Add the tomatoes and cook, covered, for about 30 minutes.

3 Remove the rabbit, then remove the meat from the bones and shred. Place the rabbit back in the saucepan and cook for 15 more minutes.

4 Cook the pasta in a large pot of boiling salted water until al dente, then drain. Place in a warmed serving bowl and toss well with the sauce. Serve with Parmigiano at the table.

Pappardelle ai Funghi

Pappardelle with Mushroom sauce

Serves 4

- 8 ounces porcini mushrooms
- 2 cloves garlic, crushed
- 2 tablespoons calamint, or substitute mint, thyme or parsley, chopped
- 6 tablespoons olive oil
- salt and pepper
- 1 large ripe tomato, peeled, seeds removed and crushed or 1 cup peeled crushed canned tomatoes
- 1 pound fresh pappardelle or tagliatelle

1 Clean the mushrooms by removing any dirt and quickly rinsing under cold water. Cut first into slices and then into squares, making sure not to cut them too small.

2 In a skillet, sauté the garlic and calamint in the olive oil until the garlic starts to turn golden.

3 Add the mushrooms and cook for 5 minutes.

4 Season with salt and pepper and add the tomatoes.

5 Cook slowly, covered, for about 20 minutes, then remove the garlic.

6 Cook the pasta in a large pot of boiling salted water until al dente, then drain. Place in a warmed serving bowl and toss well with the sauce. Serve without cheese.

These pappardelle can also be prepared "white." Instead of tomatoes, a 1/2 cup of white wine is added and once it reduces, a 1/2 cup of broth is added; cream is never used.

Pappardelle al Germano

Pappardelle with Wild Duck sauce

Serves 6

- 1 wild duck or mallard, cleaned
- vinegar
- 2 cloves garlic, finely chopped
- 2 bay leaves, finely chopped
- pinch of hot red pepper flakes
- 6 tablespoons olive oil
- 1 cup red wine
- broth
- salt
- 1 pound fresh pappardelle or tagliatelle

1 Clean the duck and remove its legs, head and neck, then remove the skin and cut into 4 pieces. Marinate the duck in a mixture of vinegar and water for a couple of hours.

2 In a saucepan, sauté the garlic, bay leaves and hot red pepper flakes in the olive oil until the garlic is just golden.

3 Add the duck and cook until it's browned. Add the wine and let it reduce. Continue to cook, adding broth (about 1 cup), until the duck is tender enough to be removed from the bone.

4 Remove from heat and remove the duck, then remove the meat from the bones and shred. Season with salt and adjust the sauce to the right consistency with broth.

5 Cook the pasta in a large pot of boiling salted water until al dente, then drain. Toss well in the sauce. Serve without cheese.

Pappardelle sulla Lepre

Pappardelle in Hare sauce

Serves 4

- 1 onion, finely diced
- 1 stalk celery, finely diced
- 1 carrot, finely diced
- 2 tablespoons parsley, finely diced
- 2 ounces pancetta, chopped
- 1/4 young hare (with heart, lungs and blood if possible), cleaned and cut into large pieces
- 6 tablespoons olive oil
- 2 cups red wine
- salt and pepper
- pinch of cinnamon
- 1 whole clove, crushed
- 1 pound pappardelle or large fresh egg tagliatelle
- grated Parmigiano-Reggiano

1 In a saucepan, sauté the onion, celery, carrot, parsley and pancetta in the olive oil until the vegetables are softened. Add the hare (along with the heart and lungs, finely chopped, if you have them) and cook for a few minutes. Add the wine (along with the blood, diluted in a little hot water, if you have it), season with salt and pepper, the cinnamon and clove and continue to cook, moistening with hot water or broth, if needed, until the hare is well cooked, about 2 hours.

2 Remove the rabbit, then remove the meat from the bones and shred. Place the rabbit back in the saucepan and cook for a few more minutes.

3 Cook the pasta in a large pot of boiling salted water until al dente, then drain. Place in a warmed serving bowl and toss with the sauce. Serve with Parmigiano at the table.

You might be surprised not to find tomatoes among the list of ingredients; it's almost always used with the pappardelle dishes prepared in restaurants, but in reality, for the hare sauce, tomatoes should be substituted with the hare's blood.
In fact, considering that this dish seems to have been popular with the Etruscans, there is absolutely no doubt that tomatoes don't matter, since this red vegetable, originating from America, didn't appear on Italian tables until after 1700. However, because blood is not easy to find, a teaspoon of tomato purée or no more than 1 cup of canned peeled tomatoes can be used instead.

Pappardelle al Sugo di mare

Seafood Pappardelle

Serves 4

- 1 clove garlic, minced
- 2 tablespoons parsley, minced, plus extra
- pinch of hot red pepper flakes
- 6 tablespoons olive oil
- 1/2 pound squid, cleaned and cut into strips
- salt
- 3 ripe tomatoes, peeled, seeds removed and diced
- 1/2 pound shrimp, shells removed
- 2 red mullet fillets
- 1 pound fresh pappardelle or tagliatelle

1 In a saucepan, sauté the garlic, parsley and hot red pepper flakes in the olive oil. Before the garlic turns golden, add the squid.

2 Season with salt and cook over high heat for 5 minutes. Add the tomatoes and cook for 10 minutes. Add the shrimp and mullet and cook for a few more minutes, until the seafood is cooked through.

3 Cook the pasta in a large pot of boiling salted water until very al dente, then drain. Toss in the sauce and sprinkle with minced parsley.

Pasta e Fagioli

Pasta and Bean soup

Serves 4

- 8 ounces dry cannellini beans, soaked overnight or 1 1/4 pounds fresh cannellini beans, shelled
- salt
- 2 cloves garlic
- 1 sage leaf, finely chopped
- 1/2 cup olive oil, plus extra
- 1 sprig rosemary, finely chopped
- pinch of hot red pepper flakes
- 4 ripe tomatoes, peeled and seeds removed
- 1/2 pound fresh maltagliati
- freshly ground pepper

Pasta and beans is the true Italian national dish. It's found in every region, even if it's done in slightly different ways. The most typical recipes are found in Tuscany, Campania and Veneto.

1 In a pot, cook the beans over low heat in 6 cups of salted water with 1 garlic clove (minced), the sage and 2 tablespoons of the olive oil until the beans are cooked through and rather soft. Reserve 4 tablespoons of the beans in the pot and puree the remaining ones in a food mill or food processor, then add the puree back to the pot.

2 In a skillet, sauté the remaining garlic clove (unpeeled and crushed), rosemary and hot red pepper flakes in 6 tablespoons of the olive oil until the garlic is just golden. Add the tomatoes, crushing them, and continue to cook for 10 more minutes.

3 Remove the garlic and pour the sauce into the pot of beans.

4 Season with salt (you can also add a little vegetable bouillon) and add the pasta. Add some water, if needed, and cook until al dente, keeping in mind that the pasta and beans should be rather thick.

5 Wait a few minutes before serving. Serve warm, but not hot, drizzled with a little olive oil and sprinkled with some freshly ground pepper. Cheese is optional; in some regions it's used, but in other places, such as Tuscany, it's not.

Pasta Stortellata o "Intordellata" alla lucchese

Pasta with Ragu, Ricotta and Swiss Chard

Serves 4

- 1 pound Swiss chard leaves
- 1 tablespoon butter
- salt
- 2/3 cup sheep's milk ricotta
- 1 pound fresh pappardelle
- Tuscan gravy (see recipe)
- grated Parmigiano-Reggiano

1 Boil the Swiss chard only in the water that remains on the leaves after washing them, then squeeze out and coarsely chop.

2 In a skillet, sauté the Swiss chard in the butter and a pinch of salt. Place them in a bowl and roughly mix with the ricotta.

3 Cook the pasta in a large pot of boiling salted water until al dente, then drain, leaving a little wet. On the bottom of a warmed serving bowl, place a layer of the gravy, followed by a layer of the pasta, a layer of the Swiss chard and ricotta mixture, another layer of gravy and Parmigiano, then another layer of pasta. Continue to make the layers in this way, ending with a layer of gravy and Parmigiano. Wait a few minutes before serving.

This delicious dish can be prepared simply by mixing together regular gravy, ricotta and chopped Swiss chard.

Pici all'

Fresh Spaghetti with Garlic sauce

Serves 6

- 4 cups type 0 flour
- salt
- 6 cloves garlic, crushed or thinly sliced
- 1 ½ cups peeled canned tomatoes, diced
- 6 tablespoons high-quality olive oil
- freshly ground pepper
- 1 ½ large ripe tomatoes, peeled and chopped or 1 ½ cups peeled canned tomatoes, chopped
- grated mature pecorino

1 Mix the flour with room temperature water and a little salt. Work together to obtain a rather firm dough (harder than bread dough).

2 Roll out the dough to about 1/8 inch thick, then cut it into strips about 1/3 inch wide.

3 Work the dough by rubbing it between your hands ("appiciare" as we say) to form long, thick spaghetti about 8 inches long and ranging from 1/8 to 1/4 inch wide (in a single pasta strand).

4 In a large skillet, sauté the garlic in the olive oil. Season with salt and pepper and cook for a couple of minutes. Add the tomatoes and continue to cook for 20 more minutes.

5 Cook the pasta in a large pot of boiling salted water for only about 5 minutes, then drain. Add to the skillet and toss in the sauce. Serve sprinkled with plenty of pecorino and some freshly grounded pepper.

A widely known variation of this recipe is called pici with "**briciole**" (**crumbs**) or with "**salsa sbriciolata**." It's made by toasting in a skillet with 5 tablespoons of olive oil, 2 garlic cloves and about 3 tablespoons dry bread that has been toasted and grounded (breadcrumbs are not good because they are too fine). Season with salt and pepper and pour the sauce over the cooked pici.

Pici con l'Anatra

Fresh Spaghetti with Duck sauce

Serves 6

- 1 white onion, finely chopped
- 1 stalk celery, finely chopped
- 2 whole cloves, crushed
- 4 tablespoons olive oil
- 2 cups vegetable broth
- 1 deboned duck, about 1 3/4 pounds, cut into thin slices
- 1 1/2 cups peeled canned tomatoes, diced
- salt and pepper
- 1 pound fresh pici

1 In a pot, sauté the onion, celery and cloves in the olive oil until the vegetables are softened, then add the broth.

2 Add the duck to the saucepan and "over-cook" for about 30 minutes, making sure it doesn't stick to the bottom of the pot.

3 Add the tomatoes and continue to cook for 15 more minutes. Remove from the heat and season with salt and pepper.

4 Cook the pasta in a large pot of boiling salted water until al dente, then drain. Toss with the sauce (with the duck pieces removed) and serve with the pasta accompanied by the duck pieces.

Pici is a kind of fresh eggless spaghetti common in Tuscany, in the Siena province, particularly in Chiusi and Chianciano; they are also typical of Montalcino, where they are called pinci. There are also similar preparations in Umbria (**ciriole**, **umbricelli**, **strengozzi**) and other southern regions. Today pici is commercially available dry or fresh, but that's quite another thing!

Pisarei e fasò alla Piacentina

Piacenza-style Pasta and Beans

Serves 6

- 8 ounces dry borlotti (cranberry) beans, soaked overnight
- 2 3/4 cups flour, plus extra
- 1/4 cup breadcrumbs
- salt
- 1 onion, finely chopped
- 1 clove garlic, minced
- 2 ounces lardo, or substitute pancetta, chopped
- 3 tablespoons olive oil
- 2 large ripe tomatoes, peeled and chopped or 2 cups peeled canned tomatoes, chopped
- pepper
- grated Parmigiano-Reggiano

1 Add the beans to a pot of cold salted water and cook until almost tender.

2 Mix the flour with the breadcrumbs, some warm water and salt and work together until a firm and elastic dough is obtained. With the help of some flour, form the dough into large tubes as thick as a pencil and cut them into pieces about 1/4 inch long. Press them using your thumb and index finger to form small shells.

3 In a large saucepan, sauté the onion and garlic in the lardo and olive oil, until the onion is just softened. Add the tomatoes, season with salt and pepper and cook for 30 minutes. Add the beans and 1 cup of their cooking water and continue to cook for about 30 more minutes.

4 Cook the pasta in a large pot of boiling salted water until al dente (it should take about 15 minutes), then drain with a slotted spoon. Place in a warmed serving bowl and toss with the sauce and plenty of Parmigiano.

Pizzoccheri della Valtellina

Valtellina Pizzoccheri

Serves 4

- 1 cup type 0 flour
- 1 3/4 cup buckwheat flour
- salt
- 1/2 pound yellow potatoes, peeled and cut into thick slices or cubes
- 1 pound white cabbage, cored and cut into thin chips
- 2 sage leaves, finely chopped
- 1 clove garlic, minced
- 1 onion, thinly sliced
- 1/2 cup butter
- 1/3 pound Fontina, grated with a large hole grater or diced
- grated Parmigiano-Reggiano

1 Sift the two flours together and mix with water and a little salt (today many people add an egg and some milk, but this isn't traditional). Work together until a smooth and firm dough is obtained. Roll out the dough rather thick and cut into large tagliatelle-like noodles, about 1/3 inch wide and about 2 1/2 - 2 3/4 inch long.

2 Add the potatoes and cabbage to 3/4 gallon (12 cups) of cold salted water. Cook for 20 minutes, then add the pizzoccheri and cook until al dente (about 12 minutes).

3 Meanwhile, in a skillet, sauté the sage, garlic and onion in the butter until the onions are browned.

4 Drain the pizzoccheri together with the potatoes and cabbage and add to a warm serving bowl. Add the butter mixture and Fontina. Toss well and let stand for 1 minute. Serve with Parmigiano at the table.

Pizzoccheri can be also be prepared in a skillet, in layers: begin with a layer of pasta and vegetables, then a layer of cheese slices dotted with melted butter, and so on, ending with a layer of pasta. It's then cooked au gratin in the oven for a few minutes.

Scialatielli ai Frutti di mare

Seafood Scialatielli

Serves 4

For the pasta:

- 1 3/4 cup type 0 flour
- 1 3/4 cup durum wheat flour
- salt
- 4 basil leaves, finely chopped
- 2 tablespoons grated pecorino dolce
- 1 egg
- 1/2 cup milk
- 1 tablespoon olive oil

For the sauce:

- 2 1/4 pounds mussels and clams
- 2 cloves garlic, minced
- 2 tablespoons parsley, minced
- pinch of hot red pepper flakes
- 6 tablespoons olive oil
- 1 1/2 large ripe tomatoes, peeled

1 Prepare a normal dough with the ingredients listed and set aside to rest wrapped in plastic wrap in the refrigerator for 30 minutes. Roll out the dough to about 1/8 thickness and cut into fettucce (flat noodles) about 1/8 inch wide. The scialatielli shouldn't be too long, about 4-6 inches in length.

2 Thoroughly clean and scrub the mussels and clams and also debeard the mussels. Add to a skillet and cook, covered, over high heat until they open (you can reserve some unopened ones for garnish). Shell the mussels and clams, reserving their water.

3 In a large, deep skillet, sauté the garlic, parsley and hot red pepper flakes in the olive oil until the garlic is golden. Cut the whole tomato in half and add all 3 tomato halves to the skillet. Cook for a few minutes, moistening with the reserved mussel and clam water.

4 Meanwhile, cook the pasta in a large pot of boiling salted water until just al dente, then drain. When the skillet liquid has reduced a little, add the pasta and the shellfish meat and toss well. Serve immediately.

Scialatielli is a homemade pasta, typical of the Amalfi Coast that looks like fettuccine, but is thicker. This pasta is a fairly recent invention (around 1960) and today is easily found in stores in both fresh and dried versions. The term "scialatielli" is derived from the word "sciglio," which is a verb in Neapolitan dialect that means "messy," referring to the pasta's resemblance to disheveled hair.

Stracci agli Asparagi

Small Lasagna with Asparagus sauce

Serves 4

- 1 1/3 pounds thin or wild asparagus
- 1 clove garlic
- 3 tablespoons olive oil
- 1/2 cup white wine
- salt and pepper
- 2 ounces fat and lean sliced prosciutto or pancetta, cut into strips
- 1 pound fresh stracci (irregular squares, about 1 1/2 inches in diameter)
- 1/4 cup butter
- grated Parmigiano-Reggiano

1 Remove the bottom tough ends of the asparagus. Cut off the tips and cut the remaining green stalks into pieces about 2 inches long, them cut each piece in half lengthwise

2 In a skillet, sauté the garlic (whole) in the olive oil until it's just golden. Add the asparagus and cook for a few minutes, then add the wine.

3 Once it reduces, moisten with some boiling water and season with salt and pepper. Continue to cook, covered, until the asparagus are somewhat tender but still a little crisp. Add the prosciutto, warming it, but not letting it cook.

4 Cook the pasta in a large pot of boiling salted water until al dente, then drain. Toss the pasta in the skillet with the sauce. Add the butter and a little of the pasta cooking water, if needed. Serve hot and creamy with plenty of Parmigiano.

Strichetti all'Aglio

Strichetti with Garlic sauce

Serves 6

- pasta dough made from 3 1/4 cups flour, 4 tablespoons grated Parmigiano-Reggiano, 4 eggs and nutmeg
- 8 cloves garlic, minced
- 3 tablespoons parsley, minced
- 6 tablespoons olive oil
- 2 large ripe tomatoes, peeled and chopped or 2 cups peeled canned tomatoes, chopped
- salt and pepper
- grated Parmigiano-Reggiano

1 Prepare a normal pasta dough with the addition of 4 tablespoons Parmigiano and a pinch of nutmeg.

2 Roll out the dough, not too thin, and, using a pasta wheel, cut into diamond shapes, about 1 inch on each side (or about 1x2 inch rectangles). Pinch together the two opposite ends (or pinch the center to form a farfalle, or butterfly, pasta shape).

3 In a saucepan, slowly sauté the garlic and parsley over low heat in the olive oil and 1 tablespoon water (the garlic should not turn golden).

4 Add the tomatoes, season with salt and pepper and continue to cook over high heat for 10 more minutes.

5 Cook the pasta in a large pot of boiling salted water until al dente, then drain. Place in a warmed serving bowl and toss with the sauce. Serve with Parmigiano at the table.

Stricchetti or strichetti or strichet are a specialty of Emilia-Romagna and are also delicious cooked in high-quality meat broth or vegetable soup; in this case, make the pasta smaller (about 3/4 x 1 1/2 inches).

Tagliatelle con l'Anguilla

Tagliatelle with Eel sauce

Serves 4

- 1 onion, finely chopped
- 1 stalk celery, finely chopped
- 1 carrot, finely chopped
- 1 clove garlic, minced
- 2 tablespoons parsley, finely chopped
- 6 tablespoons olive oil
- flour for dredging
- 1 pound eel pieces (about 2 inches in diameter each)
- salt and pepper
- 1/2 cup red wine
- 1 1/2 large ripe tomatoes, peeled and chopped or 1 1/2 cups peeled canned tomatoes, chopped
- 1 pound tagliatelle (eggless is best)

1 In a skillet, sauté the onion, celery, carrot, garlic and parsley in the olive oil for a few minutes.

2 Lightly flour the eel and add to the skillet. Sauté for a few minutes, then season with salt and pepper. Add the wine and let it reduce. Add the tomatoes and continue to cook for 30 more minutes.

3 Remove the eel from the skillet and eliminate the bones. Place back in the skillet and cook for a few more minutes, crushing the eel a little.

4 Cook the pasta in a large pot of boiling salted water until al dente, then drain. Place in a warm serving bowl and toss with the sauce.

Tagliatelle all'Astice

Lobster Tagliatelle

Serves 4

- 2 small lobsters
- ½ cup olive oil
- 2 cloves garlic, thinly sliced
- pinch of hot red pepper flakes
- salt
- ¼ cup brandy or Cognac
- 1 cup white wine
- 4 ripe plum tomatoes, peeled, seeds removed and diced
- 1 pound egg tagliatelline

1 Split each lobster in half lengthwise. Place in a large, deep skillet with 6 tablespoons olive oil, garlic and hot red pepper flakes.

2 Season with salt and slowly sauté for 5 minutes, while turning the lobster. Add the Brandy and let it reduce, then add the wine and let it reduce again.

3 Add the tomatoes and cook for 10 minutes, then remove the lobsters from the skillet.

4 Cook the pasta in a large pot of boiling salted water until very al dente, then drain. Add to the skillet and finish cooking the pasta with some water or broth and the remaining olive oil.

5 Serve hot in bowls with the lobster on the pasta.

Tagliatelle con Calamari e scampi

Squid and Shrimp Tagliatelle

Serves 4

- 1 clove garlic, minced
- pinch of hot red pepper flakes
- 6 tablespoons olive oil
- 1/3 pound small calamari or cuttlefish, cleaned and cut in half (or into pieces if large)
- 1/3 pound shrimp, tails intact, cut in half lengthwise
- 1/2 cup white wine
- 1 pound tagliatelline
- salt
- parsley, finely chopped

1 In a large skillet, sauté the garlic and hot red pepper flakes until the garlic is almost golden.

2 Add the seafood and cook for 1 minute. Add the wine and let it reduce.

3 Cook the pasta in a large pot of boiling salted water until al dente, then drain, leaving a little wet. Toss in the sauce and sprinkle with parsley. Serve immediately.

Tagliatelle ai Carciofi o "Piccagge al tocco di carciofi"

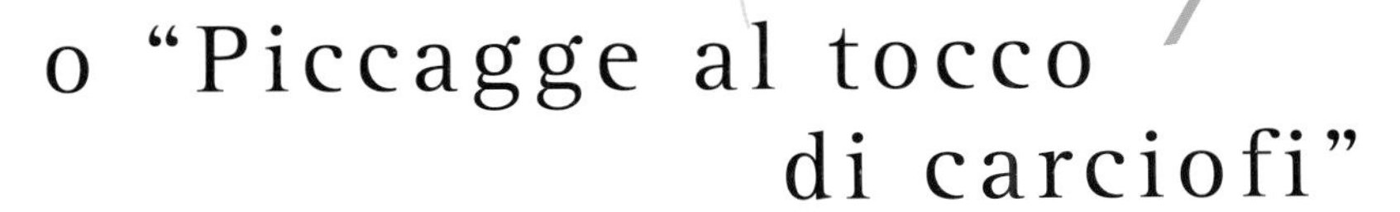

Artichoke Tagliatelle

Serves 4

- 8 small and tender artichokes
- ½ onion, finely chopped
- 1 clove garlic, minced
- 2 tablespoons parsley, finely chopped
- 6 tablespoons olive oil
- 1 large ripe tomato, peeled, seeds removed and chopped or 1 cup peeled canned tomatoes, chopped
- 1 ounce dried porcini mushrooms, soaked and chopped
- salt and pepper
- 1 tablespoon flour
- 1 pound fresh tagliatelle or pappardelle
- grated Parmigiano-Reggiano

1 Clean the artichokes by removing tough leaves, inner hairy choke and stem (leaving about 2 inches), then cut into small pieces.

2 In a skillet, slowly sauté the onion, garlic and parsley in the olive oil until almost golden. Add the artichokes and cook for 5 minutes. Add the tomatoes and mushrooms and season with salt and pepper. Continue to cook, slowly, making sure the artichokes don't become very soft.

3 Toast the flour in a small nonstick skillet so that it becomes amber in color, then add to the sauce and mix well, adding some hot water, if needed. Cook for a few more minutes, then remove from the heat.

4 Cook the pasta in a large pot of boiling salted water until al dente, then drain. Place in a warm serving bowl and toss with the sauce. Serve with Parmigiano at the table.

This is the classic recipe for Ligurian "**touch of artichokes**" In this region, tagliatelle noodles are about ½ -¾ inch wide and are called "**piccagge**" or "**picagge**" in dialect (piccagge are the ribbons used by tailors for trimming). Piccagge are usually made with durum wheat flour and fewer eggs in respect to the Emilian tradition.

Tagliatelle e Ceci o "Ciceri e tria"

Tagliatelle and Chickpeas

Serves 4

- 4 1/4 cups broth (or vegetable bouillon)
- 1 pound cooked chickpeas
- 1 stalk celery, finely chopped
- 1/2 onion, finely chopped
- 1 sprig rosemary, finely chopped
- 3/4 pound fresh tagliatelle made from durum wheat flour and water (about 2/3 inch wide)
- 1/2 cup olive oil, plus extra
- freshly ground pepper

1 Bring the broth to a boil. Meanwhile, puree half of the chickpeas. Add the celery, onion, rosemary and the whole and pureed chickpeas to the broth.

2 Shorten the tagliatelle so that it's about 4 inches long. Deep-fry half of the pasta in a skillet with the olive oil until lightly golden in color.

3 Add the remaining pasta to the broth and cook until al dente, then add the fried pasta.

4 Stir well (it should have a semi-liquid consistency) and serve immediately with plenty of freshly ground pepper and drizzled with olive oil.

This ancient dish from Salento (Lecce) seems to be one of the first examples of the use of pasta in Italy, and is typical of the feast of St. Joseph (March 19). The same pasta can also be found in Basilicata, called **"Lagane and chickpeas"** This recipe includes the addition of cherry tomatoes and the pasta isn't fried before it's boiled.

Tagliatelle con i Fagioli

Tagliatelle with Beans

Serves 4

- ½ onion, finely chopped
- 1 small carrot, finely chopped
- 1 stalk celery, finely chopped
- 6 tablespoons olive oil
- 2 ounces pancetta, diced
- 6 ounces dry borlotti (cranberry) beans, soaked in water overnight
- salt and freshly ground pepper
- 1 large ripe tomato, peeled and chopped or 1 cup peeled canned tomatoes, chopped
- 1 pound fresh egg tagliatelle or pappardelle
- grated pecorino or Parmigiano-Reggiano

1 In a pot, slowly sauté the onion, carrot and celery in the olive oil until softened. Add the pancetta and cook for a few minutes, then add the beans.

2 Season with salt and pepper, then add the tomatoes and 2 cups water. Slowly cook until the beans are fully cooked and the sauce has reduced (moisten with some water, a little at a time, as needed).

3 Cook the pasta in a large pot of boiling salted water until al dente, then drain. Place in a warm serving bowl and toss with the sauce. Sprinkle with some grated cheese and freshly ground pepper.

A similar recipe can be found in Abruzzo, called **"sagne and beans"** It uses lasagna noodles (instead of tagliatelle), made only from flour and water, which are cut ¾ inch wide, then into ¾ inch diamonds.

Tagliatelle con i Fiori di zucca

Tagliatelle with Zucchini Flowers

Serves 4

- 1 clove garlic
- 6 tablespoons olive oil
- 16 zucchini flowers, center pistils removed and finely chopped in a food processor
- pinch of saffron (about 8 pistols), dissolved in 1/2 cup hot water
- salt and pepper
- 2 egg yolks
- 1/4 cup grated pecorino or Parmigiano-Reggiano
- 1 pound fresh egg tagliatelle or taglierini
- parsley, finely chopped (optional)

1 In a skillet, slowly sauté the garlic (whole) in the olive oil until almost golden. Add the zucchini flowers and cook for a few minutes. Add the saffron water and season with salt and pepper.

2 Remove the garlic and let the liquid reduce. Add the egg yolks and cheese and combine to obtain a creamy sauce.

3 Cook the pasta in a large pot of boiling salted water until al dente, then drain. Toss in the skillet with the sauce.

4 Serve with additional cheese and some parsley, if desired.

Tagliatelle alla Grossetana

Tagliatelle Grosseto-style

Serves 4

- 20 mussels, scrubbed and debearded
- 1 clove garlic, minced
- parsley, finely chopped
- Pinch of hot red pepper flakes
- ½ cup olive oil
- ⅓ pound squid, cleaned and cut into large pieces
- ⅓ pound shrimp, shelled
- ⅔ cup shelled and parboiled peas
- salt
- 1 pound fresh egg tagliatelle

1 Cook the mussels to open them and strain their shells, reserving the water.

2 In a skillet, sauté the garlic, a little parsley and hot red pepper flakes in the olive oil until the garlic begins to turn golden. Add the squid and shrimp and cook briefly, then moisten with the mussel water and add the peas.

3 Season with salt and cook for 10 minutes, moistening with some hot water. Add the mussels (with the meat still in the shell) and some more parsley.

4 Cook the pasta in a large pot of boiling salted water until al dente, then drain. Add to the skillet and toss briefly.

For a variation on this recipe, you can add about 1 cup ripe, peeled and chopped tomatoes.

Tagliatelle alle

Tagliatelle with Walnuts

Serves 4

- 1 cup walnut halves
- 1/3 cup white breadcrumbs, soaked in water or milk
- 1/2 clove garlic (optional)
- salt
- 1/4 cup grated Parmigiano-Reggiano or pecorino (or both), plus extra
- 1/2 cup olive oil
- pepper
- 1 pound tagliatelle

1 Remove the walnut skins by blanching them in boiling water for a few minutes, then rubbing them with a towel (you can also toast them in the oven and the skins will come off easily).

2 Using a mortar and pestle or food processor, finely chop the walnuts with the breadcrumbs, garlic and a little salt (coarse, if you use the mortar).

3 Place the mixture in a small bowl and add the cheese and olive oil. Season with pepper and stir well.

4 Cook the pasta in a large pot of boiling salted water until al dente, then drain. Place in a warm serving bowl, toss with the sauce and flavor with more cheese.

This walnut sauce is typical of Liguria where it's known as "**touch of walnuts**" or "**tucco de nuxe**" For accuracy, a curd cheese called **prescinsoea** should be added (it can be substituted with yogurt).

Tagliatelle agli Ortaggi

Vegetable Tagliatelle

Serves 4

- 1 onion, finely chopped
- 6 tablespoons olive oil
- 2 zucchini, cut into slices
- 1 eggplant, cut into slices
- 1 pepper, cut into strips
- 1 carrot, diced
- 1 stalk celery, diced
- salt and pepper
- 2 large ripe tomatoes, peeled and chopped or 2 cups peeled canned tomatoes, chopped
- 1/4 cup basil, finely chopped
- 1 pound tagliatelle
- grated Parmigiano-Reggiano

1 In a saucepan, sauté the onion in the olive oil until just softened. Add the zucchini, eggplant, pepper, carrot and celery and season with salt and pepper.

2 Cook for a few minutes, then add the tomatoes and basil and continue to cook for about 40 minutes.

3 Cook the pasta in a large pot of boiling salted water until al dente, then drain. Place in a warm serving bowl and toss with the sauce. Serve with Parmigiano at the table.

This fresh and delicious recipe can vary according to tastes and the season.

Tagliatelle con Pancetta e cipolla

Tagliatelle with Pancetta and Onion

Serves 4

- 2 large white onions, thinly sliced
- 1/4 cup olive oil
- 3 ounces pancetta, finely chopped
- salt and pepper
- 1 pound fresh tagliatelle or pappardelle
- grated Parmigiano-Reggiano

1 Soak the onions in cold water for a few hours (this will make it more delicate and digestible).

2 Add the olive oil, onions and pancetta to a skillet, season with salt and pepper and slowly cook until the onions are softened but not browned.

3 Cook the pasta in a large pot of boiling salted water until al dente, then drain. Place in a warm serving bowl and toss with the sauce.

4 Serve warm with more pepper and Parmigiano.

Instead of onions, you can use large **leeks**; you can also add about 1 cup of peeled tomatoes.

Tagliatelle con Patate e cavoli

Tagliatelle with Potatoes and Cabbage

Serves 4

- 1 small bunch black cabbage (Tuscan kale), stems removed and cut into strips
- 1/4 head Savoy cabbage, cored and cut into strips
- 2 medium potatoes, peeled and cut into chunks
- salt
- 1 pound fresh tagliatelle
- olive oil
- pepper
- grated Parmigiano-Reggiano or pecorino

1 Boil the cabbage and potatoes in a large pot of salted water until almost tender. Add the pasta and cook until al dente, then drain the pot.

2 Add the cabbage, potatoes and pasta to a warm serving bowl.

3 Drizzle with a high-quality olive oil, season with salt and pepper and sprinkle with Parmigiano, then toss well.

This recipe, like other pasta and vegetable recipes mentioned here, is an attempt at blending traditional themes related to soups with dry pasta dishes.

Tagliatelle con Patate e fave

Tagliatelle with Potatoes and Fava Beans

Serves 4

- 2 medium potatoes, peeled and cut into chunks
- ½ pound shelled fresh fava beans
- salt
- 1 pound fresh tagliatelle
- olive oil
- pepper
- grated Parmigiano-Reggiano
- basil pesto (optional)

1 Boil the potatoes and fava beans in a pot of salted water until almost tender.

2 Add the pasta and cook until al dente, then drain the pot.

3 Add the potatoes, fava beans and pasta to a warm serving bowl. Drizzle with a high-quality olive oil, season with salt and pepper and sprinkle with Parmigiano or add some pesto, if desired, then toss well.

Tagliatelle con Petto di pollo e piselli

Tagliatelle with Chicken Breast and Peas

Serves 4

- ½ chicken breast
- ½ cup butter
- 1 cup shelled peas, parboiled
- salt and freshly ground pepper
- broth
- 1 pound fresh egg tagliatelle or pappardelle
- grated Parmigiano-Reggiano

1 Boil the chicken, let cool and dice. In a skillet, melt the butter, then add the chicken and peas and season with salt and pepper.

2 Cook for about 10 minutes, moistening with a little broth.

3 Cook the pasta in a large pot of boiling salted water until al dente, then drain, reserving some of the cooking water. Add the pasta to the skillet and toss for a minute, moistening with a little of the pasta cooking water (or heavy whipping cream or milk), if it's too dry. Serve immediately with plenty of Parmigiano and some freshly ground pepper.

Tagliatelle con Piccione e funghi

Tagliatelle with Squab and Mushrooms

Serves 4

- ½ onion, finely chopped
- 1 clove garlic
- 3 sage leaves
- ¼ cup olive oil
- ¼ cup butter
- 1 squab,
  about 1 pound, cleaned and cut into 4 pieces
- salt and pepper
- ½ cup white wine
- 1 cup broth, plus extra
- 8 ounces porcini mushrooms, cleaned and thinly sliced
- 1 pound fresh egg tagliatelle or pappardelle
- grated Parmigiano-Reggiano

1 In saucepan, slowly sauté the onion, garlic (whole) and sage in the olive oil and butter until almost golden. Add the pigeon and season with salt and pepper and cook well.

2 Add the wine and let it reduce, then add the broth and continue to cook until the pigeon is tender enough to be removed from the bone.

3 Remove the garlic, sage leaves and pigeon from the skillet. Carefully remove the skin and bones from the pigeon and cut the breast into pieces. Add the pigeon back to the skillet along with the mushrooms, then moisten with more broth and cook for 10 minutes.

4 Cook the pasta in a large pot of boiling salted water until al dente, then drain. Place in a warm serving bowl and toss with the sauce. Serve with Parmigiano and pepper at the table.

Tagliatelle al Ragù bianco

Tagliatelle with White Ragu

Serves 4

- 1 small onion, finely chopped
- 1 small carrot, finely chopped
- 2 sprigs rosemary, minced
- 6 tablespoons olive oil
- ¼ pound chicken breast, cut into pieces
- 1/3 pound rabbit, cut into pieces
- 1/3 pound veal, cut into pieces
- ½ cup white wine
- salt and pepper
- broth
- 1 pound fresh egg tagliatelle or pappardelle
- grated Parmigiano-Reggiano

1 In a skillet, sauté the onion, carrot and rosemary in the olive oil until the onion begins to soften. Add the chicken, rabbit and veal and brown for about 5 minutes.

2 Add the wine and let it reduce. Remove the meat from the skillet and shred, then place back in the skillet.

3 Season with salt and pepper and continue to cook for about 30 minutes, adding some broth, a little at a time, as needed. The sauce should be smooth and creamy.

4 Cook the pasta in a large pot of boiling salted water until al dente, then drain. Place in a warm serving bowl and toss with the sauce. Serve with Parmigiano at the table.

Tagliatelle alle Salsicce

Tagliatelle with Sausage sauce

Serves 4

- 2 wild boar sausages, casings removed and crumbled
- 1 pork sausage, casing removed and crumbled
- ¼ cup olive oil
- ½ cup milk
- salt and pepper
- nutmeg
- 2 egg yolks
- 1 pound fresh egg tagliatelle or pappardelle
- grated Parmigiano-Reggiano

1 Mix the two sausages together and sauté in a skillet with the olive oil.

2 Cook for 10 minutes, then add the milk and season with salt, pepper and nutmeg.

3 Continue to cook for a few more minutes, then remove from the heat. Add the egg yolks, moisten with 2 tablespoons water and mix well

4 Cook the pasta in a large pot of boiling salted water until al dente, then drain. Place in a warm serving bowl and toss with the sauce. Serve with Parmigiano at the table.

Tagliatelle con Scampi e fiori di zucca

Shrimp and Zucchini Flower Tagliatelle

Serves 4

- 1 pound medium-sized shrimp, cut in half lengthwise
- 2 cloves garlic
- 6 tablespoons olive oil
- 1/2 cup white wine
- 12 zucchini flowers, center pistils removed and cut in half lengthwise
- salt and pepper
- parsley, finely chopped
- 1 pound fresh egg tagliatelle

1 In a large, deep skillet sauté the shrimp and garlic (whole) in the olive oil for a couple of minutes.

2 Add the wine and let it reduce. Remove the shrimp from the skillet and carefully shell them and cut into small pieces. Add the shrimp back to the sauce along with the zucchini flowers.

3 Season with salt and pepper and cook for a few more minutes, moistening with a little hot water, then sprinkle with some parsley.

4 Cook the pasta in a large pot of boiling salted water until al dente, then drain. Add to the skillet and toss well with the sauce.

You can add 3 ripe tomatoes (peeled and seeds removed) and 1 zucchini (cut into matchsticks) to the sauce.

Tagliatelle alla Trabaccolara

Tagliatelle with mixed Fish sauce

Serves 4

- 1 clove garlic, minced
- parsley, finely chopped
- pinch of hot red pepper flakes
- 6 tablespoons olive oil
- 1 1/3 pounds mixed fish with bones (scorpion fish, weever, red bream, white sea bream), cleaned, scaled, gutted and fins removed
- 1 1/2 large ripe tomatoes, peeled and chopped
- salt
- 1 pound fresh tagliatelline

1 In a skillet sauté the garlic, a little parsley and hot red pepper flakes in the olive oil and cook until the garlic is just golden. Add the fish and cook for 10 minutes, moistening with water (or white wine).

2 Remove from the heat and remove the fish from the skillet, eliminating the bones and cutting into small pieces.

3 Add the tomatoes to the skillet and cook for 15 more minutes.

4 Add the fish back to the skillet and cook briefly, then sprinkle with parsley and remove from the heat.

5 Cook the pasta in a large pot of boiling salted water until al dente, then drain. Toss in the skillet with the sauce.

A lugger or bragozzo was a small fishing ship used in the northern Adriatic that was later used in the Tyrrhenian Sea by the fishermen of San Benedetto del Tronto.

Taglierini ai Calamaretti e carciofi

Taglierini with Calamari and Artichokes

Serves 4

- 2 Roman artichokes or 4 small globe artichokes
- 2 cloves garlic, minced
- parsley, finely chopped
- 1/4 cup olive oil
- salt and pepper
- 2/3 pound small calamari
- 1 pound egg taglierini or tagliatelline

1 Clean the artichokes by removing the inner hairy choke and stem (you don't need to do this if they are small), then cut into small pieces.

2 In a skillet, sauté the garlic and some parsley in the olive oil until the garlic is almost golden. Add the artichokes and season with salt and pepper. Cook over high heat, moistening with a little hot water, until tender, then remove the artichokes.

3 Add the calamari to the same skillet (with the garlic and olive oil still in it), season with salt and pepper and cook over high heat for 5 minutes.

4 Cook the pasta in a large pot of boiling salted water until al dente, then drain. Add to the skillet with the calamari and toss well. Add the artichokes and toss well again. Serve immediately with more parsley.

Taglierini agli Asparagi

Taglierini with Asparagus

Serves 4

- $1\frac{3}{4}$ pounds thin asparagus
- 1 clove garlic
- $\frac{1}{3}$ cup butter
- $\frac{1}{2}$ cup white wine
- salt and pepper
- 1 pound fresh egg taglierini
- grated Parmigiano-Reggiano

1 Remove the bottom tough ends of the asparagus. Cut off the tips and cut the remaining green stalks into pieces about 2 inches long, then cut each piece into 2 or 4 pieces lengthwise, depending on the size of the asparagus.

2 In a skillet, sauté the garlic (whole) in the butter until golden. Add the asparagus and cook for a few minutes, then add the wine. Let it reduce, then moisten with some boiling water or vegetable broth (or bouillon). Season with salt and pepper and continue to cook until the asparagus is somewhat tender but still a little crisp.

3 Cook the pasta in a large pot of boiling salted water until al dente, then drain, reserving some of the cooking water. Toss the pasta in the skillet with the sauce, moistening with a little of the pasta cooking water, if it's too dry (the sauce should be creamy). Serve hot with plenty of Parmigiano.

Taglierini Gratinati

Taglierini au gratin

Serves 4

- 2 eggs
- 1/4 cup grated Parmigiano-Reggiano
- 1/2 cup milk
- salt
- 1 pound fresh taglierini
- 6 tablespoons butter
- breadcrumbs
- 1/2 pound buffalo mozzarella

1 In a bowl, whisk the eggs together with the Parmigiano, milk and a little salt.

2 Cook the pasta in a large pot of boiling salted water until al dente, then drain. Place in the bowl, add 4 tablespoons butter and mix well.

3 Place half of the pasta in a buttered baking dish and sprinkle with breadcrumbs. Add a layer of mozzarella and cover with the remaining pasta.

4 Sprinkle with some breadcrumbs and dot with the remaining butter. Place in the oven at 425 °F until brown and crispy on top.

You can add 2 ounces diced prosciutto cotto (cooked ham) to the layer of mozzarella.

Taglierini allo Spezzatino

Taglierini with Veal Stew

Serves 4

- 1/2 onion, finely chopped
- 2 bay leaves, finely chopped
- 1/4 cup olive oil
- 1/4 cup butter
- flour for dredging
- 1 pound veal cubes
- 1/2 cup white wine
- salt and pepper
- 1 cup broth
- 1 pound fresh egg taglierini

1 In a large skillet, slowly sauté the onion and bay leaves in the olive oil and butter until the onion is almost browned.

2 Lightly flour the veal and add it to the skillet. Cook, stirring often, until browned, then add the wine.

3 Let it reduce, then season with salt and pepper and add the broth. Cook over low heat, moistening with boiling water, a little at a time, as needed, until the meat is cooked through.

4 Cook the pasta in a large pot of boiling salted water until al dente, then drain. Place in a warm serving bowl and toss with the sauce. The veal can be served as a main course.

Taglierini al

Black Truffle Taglierini

Serves 4

- 1/4 pound black truffles, cleaned and grated
- 2 cloves garlic
- 6 tablespoons olive oil
- 1 pound thin fresh egg taglierini or fettuccine
- salt
- 2 tablespoons butter
- pepper

1 Add the truffles, garlic (unpeeled) and olive oil to a skillet.

2 Season with salt and cook over very low heat for about 10 minutes (the oil should not sauté the ingredients and the garlic should not have any color), then remove the garlic.

3 Cook the pasta in a large pot of boiling salted water until al dente, then drain. Place in a warm serving bowl and combine with the butter, then the truffle sauce. Toss well and season with salt and pepper. Serve immediately.

Some people add 2 anchovy fillets packed in salt to the sauce.
As previously mentioned for the Piedmontese "tajarin," in Marche there is also a version of tagliolini made with only egg yolks (12 egg yolks per 3 1/4 cups flour).

Taglierini alle Triglie

Red Mullet Taglierini

Serves 4

- 2 cloves garlic, finely chopped
- parsley, finely chopped
- Pinch of hot red pepper flakes
- 5 tablespoons olive oil
- 1 large ripe tomato, peeled and diced or 1 cup peeled canned tomatoes, diced
- salt
- 4 medium striped red mullets, filleted (or buy pre-made fillets)s
- 1 pound fresh taglierini

1 In a large skillet, sauté the garlic, some parsley and the hot red pepper flakes in the olive oil until the garlic is almost golden. Add the tomatoes and cook for 10 minutes.

2 Season with salt and add the red mullets and cook for another 5 minutes.

3 Cook the pasta in a large pot of boiling salted water until al dente, then drain. Toss briefly in the skillet and with some more parsley.

Tajarin delle Langhe o Taglierini ai fegatini

Taglierini with Chicken Livers

Serves 4

- 1 small onion, finely chopped
- 1/3 cup butter
- 2/3 pound chicken livers, finely chopped
- salt and pepper
- 1/2 cup dry Marsala
- 1 tablespoon tomato puree
- 1 clove garlic, minced
- 1 sprig rosemary, finely chopped
- 1 pound fresh egg taglierini or tagliatelline
- grated Parmigiano-Reggiano

1 In a skillet, slowly sauté the onion in the butter until almost golden. Add the chicken livers, season with salt and pepper and cook over low heat, stirring often.

2 Add the wine and cook until it reduces. Add the tomato puree (or a little tomato paste), garlic and rosemary and cook for 5 minutes.

3 Cook the pasta in a large pot of boiling salted water until al dente, then drain, leaving a little wet. Place in a warm serving bowl and toss with the sauce. Flavor with pepper and Parmigiano.

This traditional chicken liver ragu is called "**bedside table**" in the Langhe area. It's possible to add **rabbit** livers and some fresh or dried mushrooms to it. You can also use chicken hearts, gizzards and combs. The famous "**paparele e figadini**" typical of Veneto, is a broth-based soup made with fresh egg noodles (about 1/2 pound) cooked in meat broth, to which 1/3 pound chopped chicken livers browned in butter are added.

Tajarin al Sugo d'arrosto

Taglierini with Roast Sauce

Serves 4

- 3 1/4 cups flour, plus extra
- 3 whole eggs
- 3 egg yolks
- 1 tablespoon olive oil
- salt
- roast sauce (see recipe)

1 Prepare a pasta dough with the whole eggs, egg yolks and olive oil.

2 Work together well and form the dough into a ball. Let rest in a cool place wrapped in a damp towel for a couple of hours.

3 Roll the dough out very thin, with the help of some flour. Cut the dough into very narrow strips (true tajarin should be about a little less than 1/8 inch wide). Set aside to dry on a floured cloth.

4 Cook the pasta in a large pot of boiling salted water until al dente, then drain. Place in a warm serving bowl and toss with the roast sauce.

These tagliolini are the pride of Piedmontese cuisine. This pasta is tossed with roast sauce, or with butter and cheese, or with white truffles or with a chicken liver sauce (see recipe).
Normally, they are made with the usual ratio of 1 egg per 1 cup flour, but to make them firmer, it's best to use the proportions that are given in this recipe.

Testaroli di Pontremoli

Flat Bread with Pesto

Serves 4

- 2 ½ cups type 0 flour
- salt
- genovese basil (or olive oil)
- grated pecorino and Parmigiano-Reggiano, mixed together

1 In a bowl, mix together the flour with 1 cup water and a pinch of salt until rather fluid and smooth, without lumps.

2 Heat what is called a "sottano", that's about 15 inches in diameter (the best are made of terracotta, but there are also ones in iron and cast iron) and evenly pour a ladle of the mixture on to it (each one should be about a little less than 1/8 inch high).

3 Put on the lid (well heated), called a "soprano", and cook for about 10 minutes. Remove and set aside to cool

4 Cut into diamonds or squares, about 2 inches on each side. Briefly cook in boiling salted water, then turn off the heat and leave in the water for 1 minute.

5 Drain with a slotted spoon and place in a warm serving bowl. Layer with pesto or with just olive oil and the grated cheese mixture.

I gave you this Lunigiana testaroli recipe purely for curiosity. Obviously, you cannot make it at home and almost no one makes it in Pontremoli, but fortunately, in stores handmade and vacuum packed testaroli are available. They are good, as long as you follow the directions that I have given you for cooking and flavoring them.

Tonnarelli Cacio e pepe

Cheese and Black Pepper Tonnarelli

Serves 4

- 1 pound tonnarelli (see note) or thick spaghetti
- salt
- 1½ cups freshly grated Pecorino Romano
- coarse ground black pepper

1 Cook the pasta in a large pot of boiling salted water.

2 Meanwhile, in a large serving bowl, combine the pecorino and a little ground pepper.

3 Mix well and add a few tablespoons of the pasta cooking water. Stir until there is a somewhat creamy sauce.

4 Drain the pasta, leaving it very wet, almost soupy, and transfer to the serving bowl. Toss well, evenly distributing the sauce over the pasta.

5 Serve immediately hot and sprinkled with more pepper.

Tonnarelli is a type of egg pasta from Lazio that is very similar to spaghetti or macaroni alla chitarra from Abruzzo. It's made using a wooden frame with metal wires on which the dough is placed and cut by going over it with a rolling pin. Today the pasta can be easily found ready-made, but you can substitute it with spaghetti alla chitarra (fresh is best) or with spaghettoni.

Troccoli alla Daunia

Thick cut Spaghetti Daunia-style

Serves 4

- 2 cloves garlic, thinly sliced
- 6 tablespoons olive oil
- 1 1/2 large ripe tomatoes, peeled and chopped or 1 1/2 cups peeled canned tomatoes, chopped
- salt and freshly ground pepper
- 1 pound Apulian troccoli (see note)
- 2 eggs
- 2 tablespoons grated pecorino
- 1/2 pound asparagus tips, cooked until somewhat tender but still a little crisp and chopped

1 In a saucepan, sauté the garlic in the olive oil until just golden. Add the tomatoes, season with salt and pepper and cook for about 15 minutes.

2 Cook the pasta in a large pot of boiling salted water until al dente, then drain.

3 Meanwhile, in a warm serving bowl, whisk together the eggs with the pecorino. Add the asparagus, season with salt and slowly mix together.

4 Add the pasta to the serving bowl and toss well, then add the tomato sauce and toss again. Serve with freshly ground pepper.

Tròccoli are large oval spaghetti, typical of Apulia and Basilicata (very similar to spaghetti alla chitarra), handmade with durum wheat flour, very few eggs and water. They're formed by rolling over and flattening the dough with a special rolling pin with deep grooves and made of wood or bronze that is called" torcolo," "troccolo" or "troccolaturo." Today, this type of pasta is found in stores in both fresh and dried versions. It is usually served with a braciole sauce, with mixed meats (chicken, beef, pork) or with an octopus ragu, and always with pecorino.
The recipe given here is called "Daunia, "which is the ancient name of the province of Foggia.

Trofie recchesi al Pesto

Serves 4

- 2 1/2 cups type 0 white flour (or whole wheat)
- fine salt
- 1 cup basil (about 30 leaves)
- 1/2 clove garlic
- coarse salt
- 2 tablespoons pine nuts
- 2 tablespoons grated Parmigiano-Reggiano, plus extra
- 2 tablespoons grated pecorino, plus extra
- 1/2 cup extra virgin olive oil

This recipe is also made with the addition of 2 peeled and diced yellow potatoes and about 1/4 pound green beans cooked in salted water. Just toss them with the pasta and pesto.

1 Work together the flour with a little fine salt and warm water, added a little at a time, until a smooth dough is obtained. Make the pasta by tearing off small pieces from the dough, about the size of large chickpeas. Rub each piece between the palms of your hands and form small, long corkscrew-like rods. Set aside on a towel for a couple of hours. (Fresh pre-made trofie can also be found in stores.)

2 Clean the basil leaves with a cloth (without washing them) with the stems and large ribbed parts removed. Put them in a mortar and add the garlic and coarse salt. With a pestle start to crush the ingredients against the sides with a turning motion (not up and down) until the basil is well crushed. Add the pine nuts and continue to crush. (If you don't have a mortar and pestle, you can use a food processor, but the result will not be the same.)

3 Put the pesto in a warmed bowl and add the Parmigiano and pecorino, mix well and add the olive oil in a slow, steady stream, while stirring constantly, so that you get a rather thick sauce. Cook the pasta in a large pot of boiling salted water until it floats to the surface, then drain, leaving a little wet. Place in a warm serving bowl and toss with the pesto. Serve with more grated cheese.

Vincisgrassi

Marche-style Lasagna

Serves 8

For the pasta dough:

- 3 1/4 cups all-purpose flour
- 1 3/4 cups durum wheat flour (semolina)
- 4 eggs
- 2 3/4 cups butter
- 1/4 cup dry Vinsanto or dry Marsala
- salt
- 2 tablespoons olive oil

For the sauce:

- 1 onion, 1 stalk celery, 1 carrot, finely chopped
- 1/3 pound prosciutto (fat and lean), chopped
- 1/2 cup butter
- 1 pound sweetbread, boiled and cubed
- 1/2 pound chicken giblets (combs, hearts, livers)
- white wine
- salt and pepper
- 1 cup milk

For layering the lasagna:

- 3 cups liquid-like béchamel
- grated Parmigiano
- 1/4 cup butter

1 Prepare the pasta dough. Roll out very thin and cut into rectangles, about 4x6 inches. Cook the pasta in a large pot of boiling salted water with the olive oil added to it. Drain with a slotted spoon and place briefly in cold water, then place on a damp cloth.

2 In a saucepan, slowly sauté the onion, celery, carrot and prosciutto in the butter until almost softened. Add the sweetbread and cook until browned. Add the chicken giblets, moisten with some white wine and let it reduce. Season with salt and pepper, add the milk and cook over low heat for 10 minutes.

3 Butter a baking pan with high sides and place some of the béchamel sauce on the bottom. Place a layer of lasagna noodles on top. Cover with the meat sauce, more béchamel and Parmigiano. Continue to make the layers in this way, so that they are about 1 1/2 inches high, ending with a layer of meat sauce, with béchamel and Parmigiano on top.

4 Set aside to rest of a couple of hours or more. Dot with butter and place in the oven at 400 °F for about 20 minutes. Let rest a few minutes before serving.

Recipe Index

PAOLO PETRONI is a native of Florence, where he's head of a marketing Agency. His books are known and appreciated throughout Italy as well as in the United States. The clarity and simplicity of the recipes are the force behind his publications.

Each of the recipes is carefully designed and tested in order to ensure success, eliminating long and superfluous procedures.

PAOLO PETRONI is a journalist, editor in chief of a famous Restaurant Guide and an avid wine enthusiast and gourmand. He is honorary delegate of the Florence chapter and a Secretary General of the Italian Academy of Cuisine (dell'Accademia Italiana della Cucina).

Other books from the author

IL GRANDE LIBRO DELLA VERA CUCINA TOSCANA

IL LIBRO DELLA VERA CUCINA FIORENTINA

IL LIBRO DELLA VERA CUCINA MARINARA

SPAGHETTI AMORE MIO (available also in English: SPAGHETTI, MY LOVE)